GOD'S TIMELINE

THE BIG BOOK OF CHURCH HISTORY

LINDA FINLAYSON

EARLY CHURCH   MEDIEVAL CHURCH   REFORMING CHURCH   MISSIONARY CHURCH   MODERN CHURCH

CF4•K

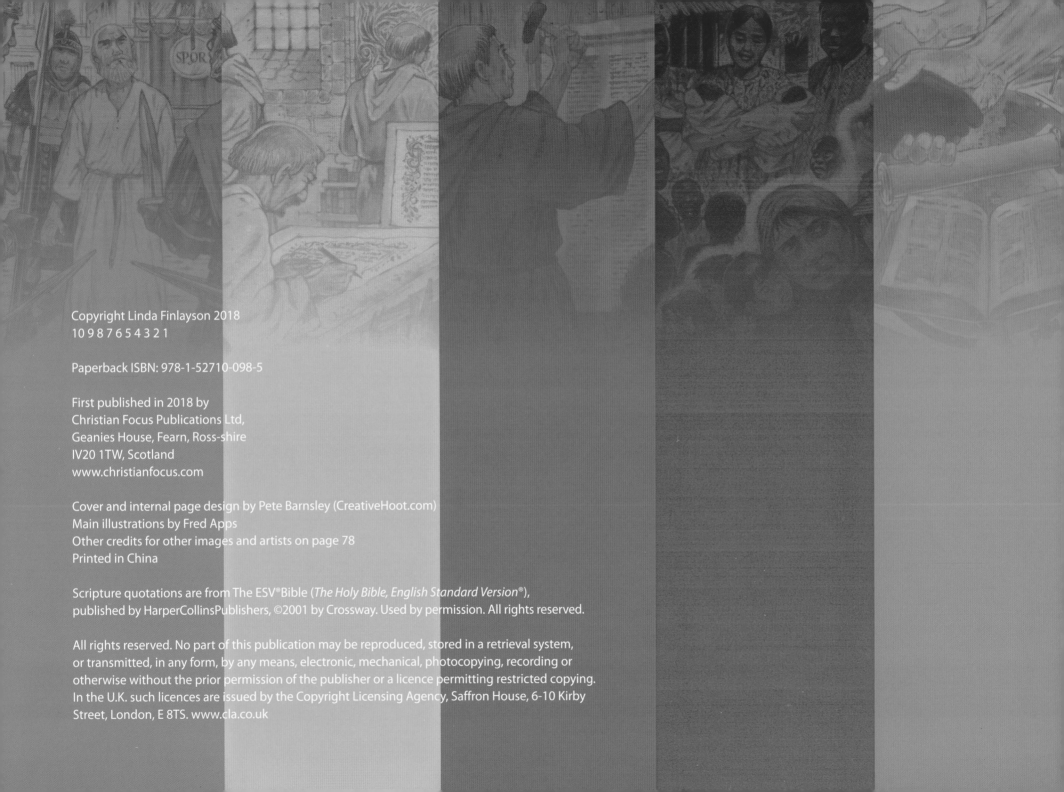

Paperback ISBN: 978-1-52710-098-5

First published in 2018 by
Christian Focus Publications Ltd,
Geanies House, Fearn, Ross-shire
IV20 1TW, Scotland
www.christianfocus.com

Cover and internal page design by Pete Barnsley (CreativeHoot.com)
Main illustrations by Fred Apps
Other credits for other images and artists on page 78
Printed in China

Scripture quotations are from The ESV®Bible (*The Holy Bible, English Standard Version*®),
published by HarperCollinsPublishers, ©2001 by Crossway. Used by permission. All rights reserved.

Linda Finlayson has done it again! She's given us a book that not only clearly describes the basic contours of Church History, but also one that draws us in with vivid illustrations and timelines. I want this in the hands of my own children and in the hands of the children of our church. I know I'll be buying copies for other friends and relatives as well. It is an excellent introduction to an important and oft-neglected topic – the work of God in the history of Christ's Church.

Jonathan Master, Professor of Theology and Dean of the School of Divinity, Cairn University. Editorial Director, Alliance of Confessing Evangelicals.

There are shelves full of books on church history, but almost all of them are directed to adults. This book not only addresses this regrettable situation, but does so with excellence. Parents, teachers and pastors who read through this engaging resource with their children will not only open their eyes to God's continuing work throughout history, but likely learn something themselves!

David Hogg, Senior Pastor, Christ Baptist Church, Raleigh, North Carolina

This book is a treasure trove of exciting stories and factual information. There is no more important and compelling story in modern history than that of the Church, the people of God saved through the work of Jesus Christ. Linda Finlayson covers 2,000 years of action-packed, global history in a way that is both clear and comprehensive. God's Timeline *should be a required text in Christian schools and in homeschooling curriculums.*

Timothy Larsen, McManis Professor of Christian Thought, Wheaton College, Wheaton, Illinois

This is a helpful and entertaining introduction to the grand sweep of church history. Not only does the text offer a fine narrative of major events and characters but the timeline is especially helpful in allowing children to visualize the interconnection of the events described. A lovely book that will be of help to Sunday school teachers and parents alike.

Carl R. Trueman, Paul Woolley Professor of Historical Theology and Church History, Westminster Theological Seminary, Philadelphia, Pennsylvania

Though regarded by some as quite humdrum and unimportant, dates and timelines are essential to the teaching of history. Erroneous dates skew everything and prevent deeper investigation of reasons and causes. This unique and creative collation of infographic timelines that map out the contours of church history is thus a welcome tool for both younger and older students of the history of God's people. The visuals and text will provide the essential foundations for deeper study in the history of the Christian Faith, and be a tremendous means of understanding the vast work of God in times past and how the Faith has been passed down to us.

Michael A.G. Haykin, Professor of Church History, The Southern Baptist Theological Seminary, Louisville, Kentucky

Linda Finlayson has written an amazing resource for families. Using clear timelines, engaging illustrations, and theological precision, God's Timeline *traces church history from its small beginnings to its worldwide impact.* The entire family can learn together about the various people, creeds, and disputes that have shaped the church for the past 2000 years.

Melissa Kruger, author *The Envy of Eve* and *Walking with God in the Season of Motherhood*

DEDICATION

For my parents, George and Irene Ginther, who have
lived their lives as examples of Christian living to their
children, grandchildren and great-grandchildren.

For my husband, Sandy Finlayson, whose continued
love and encouragement make it possible for me to
write about the things that matter.

The counsel of the Lord stands forever,
the plans of his heart to all generations.

Psalm 33:11

Your kingdom is an everlasting
kingdom and your dominion
endures throughout all generations.

Psalm 145:13

CONTENTS

PART 1
THE EARLY CHURCH 8

PART 2
MEDIEVAL CHURCH 22

PART 3
REFORMING CHURCH 34

INTRODUCTION

Welcome to your tour of Church history. You may wonder why you should read a book about people and events that happened long ago. Here's why.

History is about people and their stories, which are often filled with action and adventure. Not boring at all! We can learn a lot from how these people lived hundreds of years ago, both the good and the bad. Knowing what happened in the past can help us in the present and even into the future.

It's the same for Church history. Right from the beginning of the Early Church there were heroes, heroines and villains. We can learn from the good examples of people who chose to follow God as he commanded, and we can be warned by bad examples of what not to do. That is true throughout the history of the church, right up to modern times.

Now that you know why you should read this book, here's a little bit about how.

This book is not just about reading. It is about looking.

The first thing you will notice is that the history here has been divided up into five periods of church history:

EARLY CHURCH
MEDIEVAL CHURCH
REFORMING CHURCH
MISSIONARY CHURCH
MODERN CHURCH

Next you should notice the different logos that will appear again and again throughout these time periods. Although each time period is different from the others, there are common threads that run through all of Church History.

Here are some of the symbols you should watch for:

Councils: will appear each time the church fathers get together to discuss and decide important issues

Creeds: a vital part of the story of God's people

Martyrdom: occurs frequently throughout the church's history

Kings and Queens: appear regularly through history

Monasteries: had an important part to play

How to read the timelines. They are laid out across two pages, and they all follow the same pattern regardless of the time period. You start in the top left-hand corner and follow the arrows across the page, then down, and finally back across the page. But don't just follow the arrows! Note the people and the events, and history will unfold right in front of your eyes!

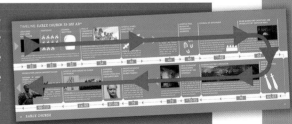

EARLY CHURCH

BEGINNING AT THE BEGINNING

Jerusalem was crowded with people from all around the Roman Empire and beyond. It was fifty days after Passover and the time for all Jews and converts to Judaism to gather for Pentecost, an annual harvest festival. But this year, 33 AD, was different from other years. Everyone was talking about the crucifixion of a man called Jesus, who had called himself the Son of God. Those who had been in Jerusalem then, recalled the sudden darkness on that day and the curtain in the temple being torn down the middle by unseen hands. And most unsettling were the stories that this man Jesus had come back to life three days after his terrible death. His followers claimed to have seen and talked to him before he rose up to heaven. Could all this be true?

Meanwhile 120 of Jesus' followers were gathered in a large house near the temple. They were praying when all of a sudden a very loud sound, like a strong wind, filled the house. As they looked around at each other they could see what looked like a tongue of flame resting on each head. But it did not burn them. Instead they were filled with the Holy Spirit and given a gift to speak in different languages. Amazed, but knowing what to do, Jesus' followers left the house and went to the temple courtyard where thousands of people were gathered for the festival. Then each one began to speak in the language they were given, telling the story of Jesus' death and resurrection and why it had to happen. Everyone standing in the temple courtyard could understand the message in their own language and were amazed. Some were frightened by this miracle, and some laughed. They

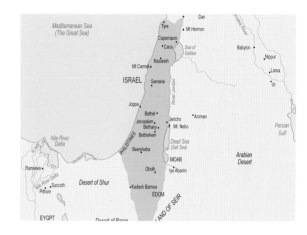

thought Jesus' followers were drunk. Then Peter stood up on a platform to speak to the entire crowd.

The throng of people quieted down and listened intently while Peter spoke. He told the story of Jesus, quoting verses from the Old Testament scriptures to show that this was all part of God's plan to save his people from their sinful condition.

Peter also told them that they were responsible for Jesus' terrible death because they had refused to listen to him and accept him as the Messiah, God's only Son. He urged them to repent of their sins and turn to God in faith, and then be baptised to show their faith publicly. The Holy Spirit gave Peter such power to speak that those that listened were convicted of their sinful hearts. That day 3,000 people believed, repented of their sins and were baptised by Jesus' apostles. That day the early church began.

TIMELINE: EARLY CHURCH 33-100 AD*

JESUS DIES AND COMES BACK TO LIFE

APOSTOLIC AGE (33-100) The time when the Apostles were alive, teaching what they had learned from Jesus. The Apostles were: James, John, Peter, Philip, Andrew, Bartholomew, Thomas, Matthew, James son of Alpheus, Thaddaeus, Simon the Zealot, Matthias and Paul.

PENTECOST

STEPHEN MARTYRED

PAUL IS CONVERTED ON ROAD TO DAMASCUS

APOSTLE PAUL (5-67 AD) was a Jew who loved God and was angry that Christians said that Jesus was God's Son. While on his way to put Christians in prison, Jesus spoke to him and changed his heart. Paul became the first missionary, traveling around the Roman Empire preaching and establishing churches. When he was put in prison, he wrote letters to the churches that are now part of our Bible.

APOSTLE JAMES MARTYRED BY KING HEROD

APOSTLE JAMES (DIED 44 AD) was a leader in the early church. He and his brother John were fishermen,

| 33 | 33 | 33 | 34 | 44 |

PERSECUTION BY ROMAN EMPERORS

EMPEROR DOMITIAN declared himself a god during his reign and commanded that all those who refused to worship him

had to be executed. He particularly wanted Jews to be killed. The next emperor, Trajan, while approving the execution of Christians, said that no one should hunt them down.

APOSTLE JOHN EXILED TO ISLAND OF PATMOS

APOSTLE JOHN: John is thought to be the last living Apostle in 90 AD. He was exiled to the island of Patmos by Emperor Domitian. While he was there, John wrote the Book of Revelation. In Revelation 2:13 & 17:6, John refers to martyrs who have died because of their faith in Jesus Christ.

EMPEROR DOMITIAN PERSECUTES JEWS AND CHRISTIANS

MOUNT VESUVIUS ERUPTS AND BURIES POMPEII

| 98-117 | ca.90 | 81-96 | 79 |

APOSTLE PAUL BEGINS HIS MISSIONARY JOURNEYS

working with their father Zebedee, when Jesus called them to be his disciples. After Pentecost, James, along with John and Peter, boldly preached the good news of Jesus Christ. King Herod Agrippa arrested James and had him executed with a sword.

COUNCIL OF JERUSALEM

COUNCIL OF JERUSALEM (CA. 49 AD) was held to settle a dispute between Jewish Christians and Gentile Christians. Some Jewish Christians thought the Gentiles should follow the Jewish law that God had given to Abraham and Moses. However, the Apostles and elders of the church decided that wasn't necessary because God had not commanded that all Christians must follow Jewish laws.

ROME BURNS AND CHRISTIANS ARE PERSECUTED BY EMPEROR NERO

EMPEROR NERO (37-68 AD) was Roman emperor for fourteen years and a thoroughly bad person. He particularly hated Christians and blamed them for a fire that destroyed much of Rome in 64 AD. As a result he had Christians rounded up and tortured and killed, and encouraged all Roman citizens to turn Christians in to the authorities. He executed the Apostles Paul and Peter.

---

44 **46** ****ca.49** **64**

ROMAN ROADS

The Roman Empire paved the way for the spread of Christianity. In each country they conquered, the Romans built wide, paved roads so their army could move from place to place easily. The Apostles and other Christians also used those roads to travel to places in the empire preaching the good news of Jesus wherever they went.

NEW TESTAMENT BOOKS ARE WRITTEN BY THE APOSTLES

THE NEW TESTAMENT: Books were written during the Apostolic Age (70 - 95 AD). They include the four Gospels about Jesus' life, the Acts of the Apostles about the early church, Paul's epistles to the churches, other letters by Apostles and the book of Revelation.

ROMANS DESTROY JERUSALEM

DESTRUCTION OF JERUSALEM (70 AD) ended a four-year Jewish revolt against the Romans. When the revolt began, Emperor Nero sent in his troops to capture the troublemakers, but it took a long time. When the Roman army finally broke through into Jerusalem, they destroyed the walls, burned the temple and killed or enslaved as many Jews as they could find. This was the end of the Jewish temple worship, and caused the Jews and Christians to scatter throughout the Roman Empire.

APOSTLES PAUL AND PETER MARTYRED IN ROME

---

ca.70-95 **70** **64, 67**

---

*AD means after the time of Jesus' birth. It is short for the Latin words Anno Domini, which means 'Year of the Lord'.

**ca. before a date means that the date is approximate.

THE FIRST MISSIONARY

Paul was born in Tarsus to Jewish parents, who named him Saul (a Jewish name). His father was also a Roman citizen, which made Saul a Roman citizen too. This became important in his later life. Like all Jewish boys then, Saul went to the synagogue school. His teachers soon realised that he was a very good student and recommended that his parents send him to Jerusalem to study with Gamaliel, a famous rabbi. Saul learned his lessons with Gamaliel well, studying the Scriptures thoroughly and worshipping God in the temple.

But while Saul was living in Jerusalem, he learned about people called Christians, who said that Jesus was the Messiah. That made Saul very angry because he didn't believe them, and he was glad when the High Priest condemned Stephen to death for preaching the Gospel. But when prisons and executions didn't stop Christianity from spreading, Saul decided to do something about it. He asked for permission to go to other cities and arrest Christians. Along with permission, Saul was also given some soldiers to help him.

Saul thought he could stop Christianity from spreading, but…

Around 34 AD when Saul was on his way to the city of Damascus, God stopped him with a light shining down on the road. It was so bright that Saul was blinded for three days.

Then Jesus spoke to Saul and he became a Christian. At first the Christians he had been persecuting didn't believe Saul had been converted and were still frightened of him. But eventually they realised that God had truly changed Saul.

God sent Saul on missionary journeys around the Roman Empire to preach the Gospel and start churches. Around this time Saul changed his name to Paul, a Greek name that Gentiles (non-Jews) would understand better. In 46 AD he went from the city of Antioch to the island of Cyprus and to cities in Asia Minor. In 50 AD he started out on his second journey from Jerusalem: up through Asia Minor to more cities than before. He crossed the water to Macedonia where he visited cities as he travelled south to Corinth, then crossed the water again to Ephesus, and finally sailed across the Mediterranean Sea to Jerusalem. His third journey in 52 AD followed some of the same route so that he could visit the churches he had established in each city to teach and encourage them.

Paul's missionary work wasn't easy. Jews in many of the cities he visited tried to stop him by having him arrested, beaten and threatened with death. Roman governors and soldiers agreed to persecute Paul to keep the Jewish leaders happy. However, Paul reminded them that he was a Roman citizen and that they couldn't arrest him without good cause or beat him without a fair trial.

Paul's final journey was not one he had planned to take. In 57 AD he was arrested in Jerusalem by the Jewish leaders. They took him to the Roman governor, who put him in prison for several years. Then, by reminding the governor and King Agrippa that he was a Roman citizen, he was sent on his final journey across the Mediterranean Sea to Rome. Once more Paul sat in prison for some time, but he used his time wisely. He wrote letters to all the young churches he had established, teaching them right doctrine, correcting those who misbehaved and encouraging them all to live as God commanded them. Finally, Emperor Nero, who hated Christians, had Paul put to death. God had used Paul to spread the Gospel to almost every part of the Roman Empire in just twenty years.

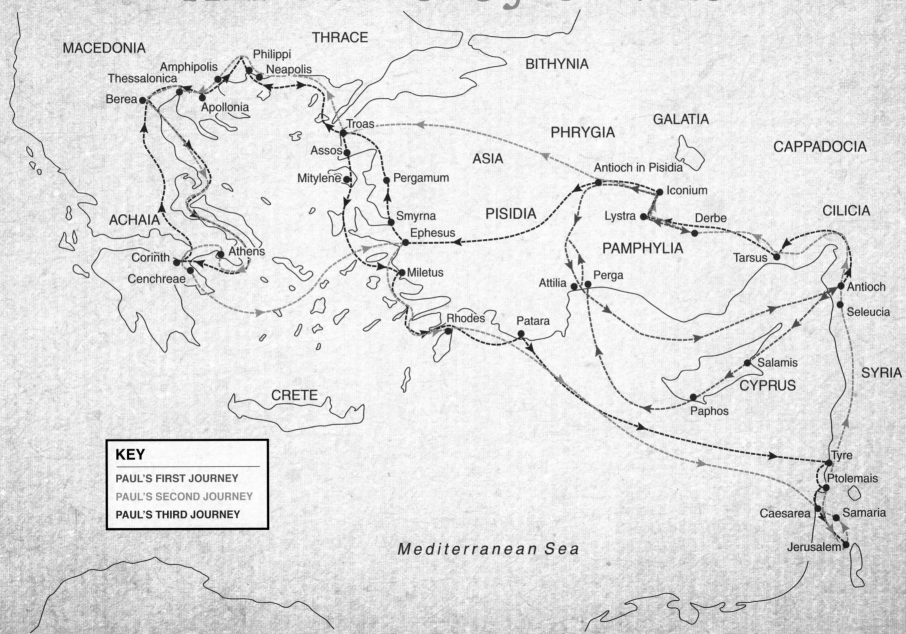

MAP OF PAUL'S JOURNEYS

MACEDONIA

THRACE

BITHYNIA

Philippi
Amphipolis
Neapolis
Thessalonica
Berea
Apollonia

GALATIA

CAPPADOCIA

PHRYGIA

Troas

Assos

ASIA

Antioch in Pisidia

Mitylene

Pergamum

Iconium

ACHAIA

Smyrna

PISIDIA

Lystra

Derbe

CILICIA

Ephesus

Athens

Corinth

Miletus

PAMPHYLIA

Tarsus

Cenchreae

Attilia

Perga

Antioch

Seleucia

Rhodes

Patara

Salamis

SYRIA

CRETE

CYPRUS

Paphos

Tyre

Ptolemais

Caesarea

Samaria

Jerusalem

Mediterranean Sea

KEY

PAUL'S FIRST JOURNEY

PAUL'S SECOND JOURNEY

PAUL'S THIRD JOURNEY

POST-APOSTOLIC AGE

POST APOSTOLIC AGE (100-199) It began with the death of the last Apostle, John, in Ephesus around 100 AD, although there was overlap. The church leaders who took over had been taught by the Apostles and spoke with the same authority.

CHURCHES ESTABLISHED IN ALMOST EVERY CITY PAUL HAD VISITED AS WELL AS IN EGYPT AND COASTAL NORTH AFRICA

CLEMENT OF ROME (DIED CA.99) was a student of the Apostle Peter, and later became bishop of the churches in Rome.

IGNATIUS OF ANTIOCH MARTYRED

IGNATIUS (DIED CA. 110) was a student of the Apostle John and Bishop of Antioch, a very large and important city. Ignatius wrote letters to various churches, encouraging and correcting them. He was arrested for refusing to worship idols and taken to Rome where he was martyred.

100-199 ···▶ ······▶ **100** ···▶ ······▶ **ca.110**

EDICT OF MILAN

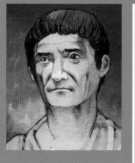

EDICT OF MILAN (313): Emperor Licinius (eastern empire) and Emperor Constantine (western empire) together issued a decree that ended persecution of Christians. The edict also said that any property that had been taken from Christians must be returned to them.

DIOCLETIAN DIVIDES EMPIRE INTO EAST AND WEST

PERSECUTION UNDER EMPEROR DIOCLETIAN BEGINS

EMPEROR DIOCLETIAN (244-311) In 303 Emperor Diocletian passed laws against Christians. Unless they recanted their beliefs and sacrificed to the Roman gods, they lost their right to own property or possessions and were arrested, imprisoned or executed. Churches were destroyed, books were burned and bishops were rounded up and imprisoned. However, instead of weakening the church, the church grew stronger than ever.

CYPRIAN IS MARTYRED

CYPRIAN (200-258) was a Bishop of Carthage in North Africa. In 249 he went into hiding during Emperor Decius' persecution of Christians. He returned to his church after the persecution stopped. In 258 when the persecution started

313 ◀··· ◀······ **285** ◀··· ◀······ **284** ◀··· ◀······ **258**

PERSECUTION UNDER ANTONINUS PIUS

MARCION EXCOMMUNICATED FOR REJECTING THE OLD TESTAMENT

MARCION OF SINOPE (85-160) Marcion taught that the God of the Old Testament was not the true God, and had nothing to do with Jesus. He also taught that only Paul's epistles were the true Scriptures. This was a heresy and the church leaders in Rome excommunicated him in 144.

POLYCARP OF SMYRNA MARTYRED

POLYCARP (CA.70-155) was a student of Ignatius and became Bishop of Smyrna. He lived a long life and provided leadership in the churches in Asia Minor. When he was 86 he was arrested and taken to the arena, where he was given a choice: deny Christ and live or remain true to Christ and die. He chose death rather than 'deny the King that saved me.'

JUSTIN MARTYR PUT TO DEATH

JUSTIN MARTYR (DIED 165) a philosopher and a Christian apologist. He was arrested while in Rome with some friends. They all refused to deny Christ and were put to death.

139-161 · · · · · 144 · · · · · 155 · · · · · 165

again, he stayed in Carthage and faced Emperor Valerian's soldiers. He was arrested and beheaded.

PERSECUTION OF CHRISTIANS WORSENS UNDER EMPEROR DECIUS

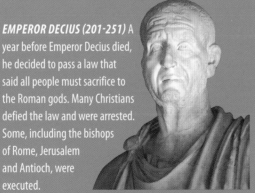

EMPEROR DECIUS (201-251) A year before Emperor Decius died, he decided to pass a law that said all people must sacrifice to the Roman gods. Many Christians defied the law and were arrested. Some, including the bishops of Rome, Jerusalem and Antioch, were executed.

BISHOP OF ROME GAINING PREDOMINANCE AMONG BISHOPS

APOSTLES' CREED

I believe in God the Father Almighty,
Maker of heaven and earth.

I believe in Jesus Christ, his only Son, our Lord,
who was conceived by the Holy Spirit,
and born of the virgin Mary.
He suffered under Pontius Pilate,
was crucified, died, and was buried;
he descended into hell.
The third day he rose again from the dead.
He ascended into heaven

258 · · · · · 250 · · · · · 200 · · · · · ca.180

DYING FOR GOD

What is a Martyr? Martyrs are people who chose to be put to death rather than give up their belief in Jesus Christ as their saviour.

Back in Early Church days, becoming a Christian was a dangerous thing. The Jewish leaders persecuted the earliest Christians because they did not think that Jesus was the Messiah that God had promised them in the Old Testament Scriptures. So they tried to stamp out Christianity right at the beginning by killing Stephen (Acts 7) and the Apostle James (Acts 12:1-2), and putting many others in prison.

At first the Roman government didn't think about Christians very much since they were just a small group of people. But by the time the Apostle Paul arrived in Rome to be tried by Emperor Nero, Christianity had spread to many parts of the empire.

Christians stood out because of their beliefs and behaviour.

1. Christians only believed in one God and refused to worship any of the Roman gods.

2. Christians welcomed all people, whether they were rich or poor, if they believed that Jesus was the Son of God; and they took care of each other.

During the second and third centuries, and into the 4th century (100-314), many Christians were martyred because they refused to stop being Christians and worship the Roman gods. Even when they were threatened with terrible ways to die, God gave them strength to stand firm in their faith.

The testimony of these martyrs had a strong influence on the whole church in the following ways.

Role models: As many Christians heard about those who had gone bravely to their death, they prayed for strength to follow their example. If Bishop Polycarp refused to recant his faith in Christ, then they too should stand strong regardless of how badly they were treated.

Encouraged the faithful to persevere: All Christians knew that they too could face persecution or death at any time. They knew it was important to keep on studying the Scriptures, praying and meeting with other Christians to worship God and celebrate the sacraments even when they were afraid.

Conversions of those who witnessed the martyrdoms: Many people watched as the martyrs were burned, stabbed, beheaded or torn apart by lions. Some laughed and enjoyed the terrible events, but others were impressed that Christians believed something so completely that they would suffer and die. These people wanted to know more about this Jesus that Christians loved so dearly, and some became Christians themselves.

After the persecutions stopped in the 4th century, the martyrs were still treated with great respect. Even though they were no longer alive, people didn't want to forget them. So they built shrines by their tombs and people could come there to remember and pray. At first this seemed like a good thing to do, but as time went on some people began to think that the martyrs had extra special power in heaven to hear their prayers and answer them. This led some people to think they could not pray directly to God, but had to ask a martyr to approach God for them. This caused some to stray from the truths of Scripture.

Almost right from the beginning of the church, some people tried to change the teachings of Jesus and lead God's people away from the truth. So the Apostles and the church leaders who came after them were careful to teach the truth and call all those who taught wrong doctrine false teachers or heretics. Here are some of the heresies:

Gnosticism: Gnostics were people who thought they had special knowledge. The Greek word *gnosis* means knowledge of spiritual matters. Their 'special knowledge' said that Jesus was not God, but only a special teacher sent from God. Jesus could not be the Son of God because he had a human body. Gnostics thought that our bodies were evil. They refused to believe that God could come in human form, even though the Bible teaches that very thing in John 1:14.

Arianism: This heresy began around 320 AD when Arius, a priest in Alexandria, began to teach that God created Jesus as a special being but he was not God. That was one of the reasons for the Nicene Creed that was written in 325. The bishops of the church wanted Christians to be very clear that Jesus is God's Son, so they wrote this:

> I believe in one God, the Father Almighty, Maker of heaven and earth, and of all things visible and invisible. And in one Lord Jesus Christ, the only-begotten Son of God, begotten of the Father before all worlds; God of God, Light of Light, very God of very God; begotten, not made, being of one substance with the Father, by whom all things were made...

GETTING IT WRONG

Marcionism: Marcion lived in Asia Minor during the early to middle part of the 2nd century. He was excommunicated in 144 AD because of strange doctrines he began to tell others. He believed that there were two gods, one in the Old Testament who was always angry and punishing people, and Jesus Christ, who was loving, and came to save his people. Marcion was wrong. The Old Testament shows many times that God was merciful to his people and even sent his prophets to other nations to call them to repentance. This same God sent his Son Jesus to die in our place so that we might be saved.

Manichaeism: Mani was born in the 3rd century in Persia (Iran). He said he had been told by God himself that the struggle between good and evil began before creation and God had lost parts of himself and was no longer omnipotent. These parts, or points of light as Mani called them, were captured in our human bodies. He designed a complicated religious programme for people to help free these points of light (the good) from the body (the evil). It was a long list of dos and don'ts that made people feel that they were earning their salvation. The Bible teaches that God is all powerful and in control of all things. People are sinful and cannot make themselves good by following rules. Only God can take away the sin in us and make us good.

Pelagianism: Pelagius lived in Rome during the 5th century. He did not believe in original sin. He taught that everyone was born good just like Adam and Eve before the Fall. When Adam and Eve sinned, they only hurt themselves, and their sin did not affect all the people who have been born since. He also said that everyone had the free will to choose to do good and follow God's commands, or choose to do evil and reject God. However, the Bible teaches us that we are all born sinful and everyone needs God's grace to be saved because we cannot do it on our own.

TIMELINE: EARLY CHURCH 315-500

ARIAN CONTROVERSY BEGINS

FIRST MONASTERY FORMED IN EGYPT

BEGINNING OF MONASTERIES: Monasteries were made up a group of buildings where men came to live to pray and worship God away from other people. Women also gathered in convents to do the same. They thought that this is the best way serve God. After St Anthony became a hermit in the desert, St Pachomius set up the first monastery in Egypt.

EMPEROR CONSTANTINE UNITES THE EASTERN AND WESTERN EMPIRE

COUNCIL OF NICAEA

COUNCIL OF NICAEA (325) was held to answer the heretical teaching of Arius. The church leaders (bishops) gathered to discuss his teachings and compare them with Scripture. The debate lasted a month, while those who supported Arius argued that he was right. In the end the bishops voted against Arius and wrote the Nicene Creed, which contains what a Christian should know and believe about God.

ATHANASIUS BECOMES BISHOP OF ALEXANDRIA

SCROLLS BEGIN TO BE REPLACED BY CODEX (BOOK)

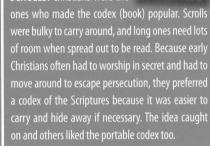

CODICES SLOWLY REPLACE SCROLLS: Christians were the ones who made the codex (book) popular. Scrolls were bulky to carry around, and long ones need lots of room when spread out to be read. Because early Christians often had to worship in secret and had to move around to escape persecution, they preferred a codex of the Scriptures because it was easier to carry and hide away if necessary. The idea caught on and others liked the portable codex too.

ATHANASIUS WRITES A PASTORAL LETTER LISTING THE CANON OF THE NT

BISHOP ATHANASIUS WRITES A PASTORAL LETTER LISTING THE CANON OF THE NEW TESTAMENT (367) This is the first time that the list of the books in the New Testament is published.

315 ▸ **320** ▸ **324** ▸ **325** ▸ **328** ▸ **360** ▸ **367**

ANTHANASIAN CREED

ANTHANASIAN CREED (500) made a clear statement about the Trinity, an important Christian doctrine:

...That we worship one God in Trinity, and Trinity in Unity, neither confounding the Persons, nor dividing the Substance. For there is one Person of the Father, another of the Son, and another of the Holy Ghost. But the Godhead of the Father, of the Son, and of the Holy Ghost, is all one, the Glory equal, the Majesty co-eternal. Such as the Father is, such is the Son, and such is the Holy Ghost.

FALL OF THE ROMAN EMPIRE

FALL OF THE ROMAN EMPIRE (476): The western part of the Roman Empire crumbled away as various tribes outside the empire invaded and took possession of territory. The final event was the invasion of Rome itself. While these events were terrible for people living in the empire, it did provide an opportunity for the church to preach the Gospel to the invaders. This event is also considered the end of ancient history.

COUNCIL OF CHALCEDON

ATTILA THE HUN ATTACKS THE ROMAN EMPIRE

COUNCIL OF EPHESUS

PATRICK BEGINS HIS MISSIONARY WORK IN IRELAND

PATRICK (CA.387-CA.461) was converted to Christianity after he was captured and enslaved by Irish pirates. Later, after he escaped, he studied to become a priest and later a bishop. He returned to Ireland as a missionary, spending the rest of his life preaching the Gospel and founding churches.

500 ◂ **476** ◂ **451** ◂ **441** ◂ **431** ◂ **ca.430**

Athanasius listed only the books written by the Apostles because these books were divinely inspired. Other Christian writings were useful, but were not part of the Scriptures.

BASIL THE GREAT BECOMES BISHOP OF CAESAREA

COUNCIL OF CONSTANT-INOPLE

JEROME BEGINS TRANSLATING THE BIBLE

JEROME TRANSLATES THE BIBLE (382-405): Jerome, a monk and a scholar, was commissioned by the Bishop of Rome to make a better translation of the Bible into everyday Latin for the church. Latin was the language most people spoke at that time. He completed the New Testament first and then went on to do the Old Testament. His translation was called the Vulgate, which means 'common speech'.

CONVERSION OF AUGUSTINE

AUGUSTINE (354-430) was a gifted teacher and orator. He was converted to Christianity in 386 and left his brilliant career in the Emperor's court behind. He returned to North Africa where he was ordained a priest and later a bishop. His writings have been influential in the church to this day.

COUNCIL OF MILAN

367   **370**   **381**   **382**   **386**   **390**

AUGUSTINE BEGINS WRITING *THE CITY OF GOD*

ROME IS CONQUERED BY ALARIC I

JEROME COMPLETES THE VULGATE

COUNCIL OF CARTHAGE

ROMAN EMPIRE DIVIDED INTO EAST AND WEST

ROMAN EMPIRE DIVIDED INTO EAST AND WEST (395): The Roman Empire was divided when Emperor Theodosius died. In his will he left the empire to his two sons, who each became emperors of their half of the empire. This also led to the beginning of the split between the eastern and western church.

COUNCIL OF HIPPO SETS THE CANON OF THE BIBLE

COUNCIL OF HIPPO (393): The bishops of the church gathered in Hippo, North Africa, to discuss several matters. The most important one that was decided was what books would be included in the Bible and which would not. The Old Testament had been decided on before Jesus was born, but the New Testament had to be firmly set so that there was no question about them. The list of twenty-seven books was approved and approved yet again at the Council of Carthage in 398.

LIBRARY AT ALEXANDRIA DESTROYED

ca. **411**   **410**   **405**   **398**   **395**   **393**   **391**

THE TWO C'S

COUNCILS:

Church leaders gather to discuss church matters and make decisions for the whole church.

The first council was held in Jerusalem (Acts 15). The Apostles and other leaders gathered to decide if Gentile Christians had to follow the Jewish laws listed in the Old Testament. They decided no, saying that all Christians must worship only God and live according to His commandments.

During the early church time period it was important to hold quite a few councils. After the persecutions had stopped in 313 with the Edict of Milan, the church leaders wanted to make sure that all Christians were worshipping correctly and being taught right doctrines. The meetings took place in different cities to make sure that all leaders could attend them. They gathered to deal with heresies that had sprung up, such as Arianism, and wrote creeds explaining correct doctrine. They also decided on important issues such as what books were inspired and belonged in the Bible. It is important to remember that the church leaders spent a lot of time studying the Scriptures and praying, asking the Holy Spirit to give them wisdom to make right decisions.

CREEDS:

The word creed comes from the Latin word *credo*, which means I believe. The councils used this word Creed as a description of the summaries of Biblical truth. Here are some of the creeds that the early church used.

Apostles' Creed (ca.180) is a short summary of the teachings of the Apostles about the Christian Faith. It was not written by the Apostles themselves. No one person has ever been named as its author. It was first called the Apostles' Creed in 390 AD and has been used since the beginning to teach new converts and remind mature Christians of what they believe.

NICENE CREED (325):

was written at the Council of Nicaea to answer the heretical teaching of Arius. It is in the same form as the Apostles' Creed but longer, with more explanations about who God is.

CHALCEDONIAN CREED:

was written to state clearly that Jesus had two natures, human and divine, and was one person. This was to answer those people who questioned how Jesus could have two natures. They insisted that he could only have one, which is wrong.

CREED OF JERUSALEM:

was a short one-sentence creed, most often said at baptisms. I believe in the Father, and in the Son, and in the Holy Ghost, and in one Baptism of repentance.

ATHANASIAN CREED:

was written to explain more clearly the Trinity, one God in three persons.

WHAT IS A CANON?

Our English word canon comes from two ancient words:

- a Greek word *kanon*, meaning rule or measure

- a Hebrew word *keneh*, which means 'standard of measurement'

When we put the meaning of the Greek and the Hebrew words together, our English word canon means a standard list or set of rules. When we use the word in describing the Bible, we mean that the Bible contains the canon or authorised list of books of the Bible.

OLD TESTAMENT

The Old Testament books were written in the Hebrew language over many centuries. As they were gathered together the books were put into categories: the Law or Torah, Historical books, Poetic or Wisdom literature and the Prophets. The Law or Torah are the first five books written by Moses: Genesis, Exodus, Leviticus, Numbers and Deuteronomy. Next are twelve historical books: Joshua, Judges, Ruth, 1 & 2 Samuel 1 & 2 Kings, 1 & 2 Chronicles, Ezra, Nehemiah and Esther. They tell the history of Israel.

Job, Psalms, Proverbs, Ecclesiastes and the Song of Solomon are the wisdom literature or poetic books. And all of the prophets' writings (Isaiah, Jeremiah, Lamentations, Ezekiel, Daniel, Hosea, Joel, Amos, Obadiah, Jonah, Micah, Nahum, Habakkuk, Zephaniah, Haggai, Zechariah and Malachi) are gathered at the end. Put these all together and you have thirty-nine books.

Sometime after the last of the books was written, about 400 years before Jesus was born, the books were all gathered together and called the canon. This is what we call the Old Testament today.

NEW TESTAMENT

The New Testament books are centred on the life and work of God's Son, Jesus, and letters of instruction and encouragement for the church. God inspired men to write the Gospels (Matthew, Mark, Luke and John), the history of the early church (Acts of the Apostles) and letters (Romans, 1 & 2 Corinthians, Galatians, Ephesians, Philippians, Colossians, 1 & 2 Thessalonians, 1 & 2 Timothy, Titus, Philemon, Hebrews, James, 1 & 2 Peter, 1, 2 & 3 John and Jude). Finally he gave the Apostle John a prophetic vision of Heaven and the end times which he wrote down in the book of Revelation.

HOW WE GOT OUR BIBLE

As had happened with the Old Testament books, these books and letters were read out to people who gathered together to worship God on the first day of the week. Copies were carefully made so that the churches in each city could have their own. However, there were also other good books that tried to encourage the early Christians in much the same way Christian books do today. But that didn't mean they should be part of God's Word. So the early church had some careful work to do to determine which books should be part of the canon of the New Testament and which should not.

Bishop Athanasius was the first to issue a list of the canonical books of the New Testament in a letter to the churches. As a church leader he spoke with authority and the churches needed to listen. Later at the Council of Hippo and also at the Council of Carthage, the bishops, after much prayer and discussion, said that Athanasius' list was correct. Only books written by the Apostles and Luke were inspired and part of the canon of the New Testament.

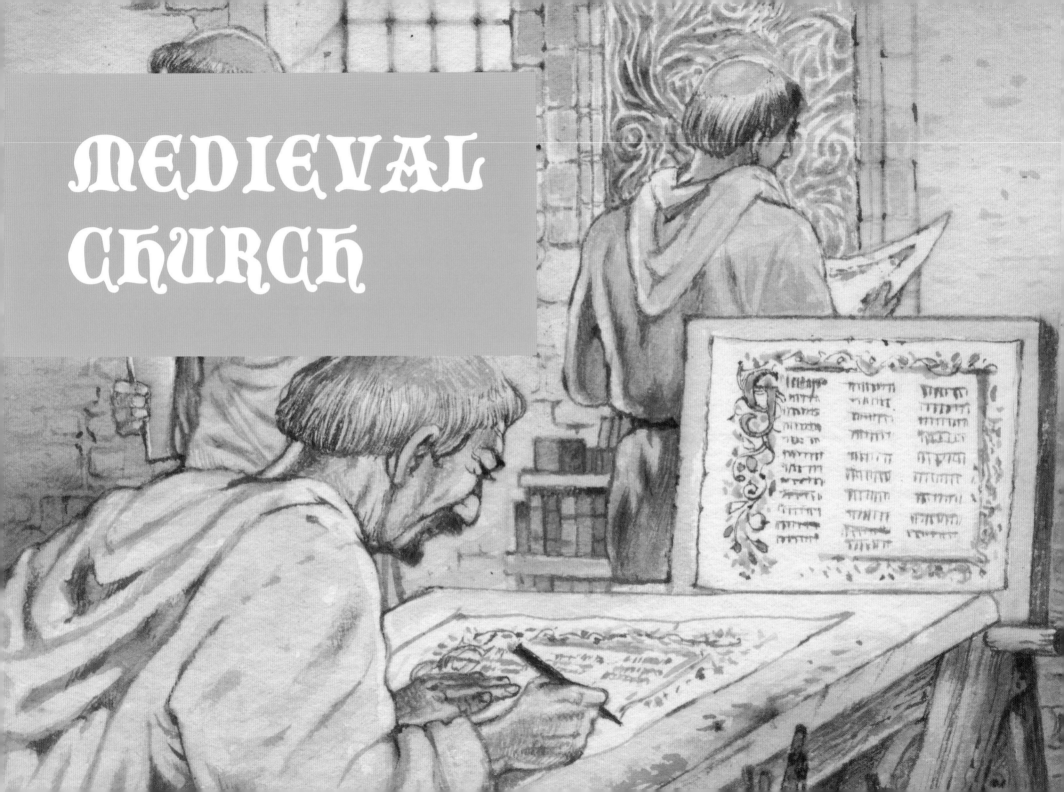

MEDIEVAL CHURCH

THE LONG-HAIRED KING

lovis was born into the Merovingian royal family around 465. They were a warrior family, always looking to expand their territory. Childeric, his father, spent most of his life waging battles against the Visigoths and the Saxons. He died when Clovis was fifteen years old, leaving Clovis the kingdom of Austrasia, what we call Belgium, Luxemburg and western Germany today. King Clovis was very much like his father. He wore his long hair in braids, which was a sign of royalty then. He began waging war on the rest of the Frankish tribes in what we now call northern and western France, defeating them one by one in many battles throughout his lifetime. He was not kind to his enemies, executing them in brutal ways. Like his father before him, Clovis worshipped pagan gods.

In 493 AD Clovis married Clotilde, a princess from the Burgundian tribe. Clovis thought it would be good to have close ties with the Burgundian king since his lands were next to Clovis' kingdom, but he didn't count on his wife changing so much in his life.

Clotilde was a Christian, the only one in her family. The official religion of the Burgundians was Arianism, the heresy first taught by Arius way back in 320 AD. Her uncle, the Burgundian king, didn't care much about religion so he allowed a Christian bishop into his court to teach the young ladies, and Clotilde was converted. Right from the start, Clotilde witnessed to her husband, urging him to give up his pagan gods and turn to the only true God. At first, Clovis refused. He even refused to allow his first son to be baptised, but Clotilde went ahead and asked Bishop Remy to do it in secret. Unfortunately their son died shortly afterwards, which made Clovis angry.

Clotilde continued to witness to Clovis, his sister and the rest of the court. She had their second son baptised without Clovis knowing, and this son lived. How much Clotilde must have praised God for that!

In 496 Clovis prepared for yet another battle by sacrificing to his pagan gods as usual, asking them to give him success. The battle did not go well. Clovis and his army were losing badly. In desperation, Clovis decided to pray to the Christian God. After much effort, the battle finally turned in Clovis' favour and they won. Clovis was convinced that God had given him the victory and he returned home to Paris to tell Clotilde that he wanted to become a Christian. Clovis' sister was also converted during that time, and many of his warriors were baptised along with Clovis, and his sister. The Frankish kingdom slowly became a Christian nation.

While it was wonderful for Clovis himself to become a Christian, it was also wonderful for the spread of Christianity. As he defeated various tribes who followed Arianism, he brought the teaching of Jesus Christ to his new citizens. The church leaders supported Clovis, and the emperor of the eastern part of the old Roman Empire, now called Byzantium, gave Clovis the honorary title of Consul.

Map of Europe from the Middle Ages

CLOVIS' CONVERSION

COUNCIL OF ORLEANS

Orleans in France, today

COUNCIL OF ORLEANS was called by King Clovis in 511. He invited thirty-three bishops to discuss rules for behaviour of the people, the king and the church. It was the first formal agreement between a king and the church.

JUSTINIAN, EMPEROR OF BYZANTIUM (EASTERN EMPIRE)

JUSTINIAN, EMPEROR OF BYZANTIUM (483-565) Justinian became emperor of the eastern or Byzantium Empire in 527 and ruled for thirty-eight years. He expanded his empire by defeating the Goths and Visigoths, and is most famous for the Justinian Code, a set of laws that gave protection to the ordinary citizen. He built many churches including the Hagia Sofia, a magnificent church in the centre of Constantinople.

BENEDICT FOUNDS MONASTERY AT MONTE CASSINO; JUSTINIAN CODE INTRODUCED

ETHIOPIAN MONKS TRANSLATE BIBLE INTO THEIR OWN LANGUAGE

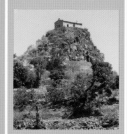

BUBONIC PLAGUE

BUBONIC PLAGUE (542-594) was also called the Justinian plague because it began when Justinian was emperor. The plague, the first known pandemic, was thought to have begun in Ethiopia or Egypt and spread to Europe and Asia through trading ships.

497 ⋯ **511** ⋯ **527-565** ⋯ **529** ⋯ *ca.* **540** ⋯ **542-594**

OTTO I MADE HOLY ROMAN EMPEROR BY POPE JOHN XII

ALFRED THE GREAT CAPTURES LONDON AND SIGNS TREATY WITH DANES

THE ALFRED PLAQUE

This plaque was erected in 1966 to mark the eleven hundredth anniversary of King Alfred's resettlement of the Roman city of London in 886, after the abandonment of the Saxon town which had existed for some three centuries in the Strand area to the west of the City. At this place a harbour and market were established by 899 to restore trade after the Viking invasions.

Erected by the Museum of London and Water City of London Properties and unveiled by The Rt. Hon. The Lord Mayor, Sir David Rowe-Ham, G.B.E. on 25th November, 1986.

TREATY OF VERDUN

Map of France from the Middle Ages

THE TREATY OF VERDUN (843) divided the Carolingian Empire between Charlemagne's sons.

VIKING, MAGYAR AND MUSLIM RAIDS THROUGHOUT EUROPE

CHARLEMAGNE CROWNED HOLY ROMAN EMPEROR BY POPE LEO III

CHARLEMAGNE (742-814) waged fifty-three wars during his lifetime, expanding the borders of the Frankish kingdom. He came to Pope Leo III's aid when a rebellion in the city of Rome threatened his life. Charlemagne's army put down the rebellion. In gratitude, Pope Leo III crowned Charlemagne 'Noble Emperor' or 'Holy Roman Emperor'.

Once more the king and the pope were partners, becoming involved in each other's business.

ICONOCLASTIC CONTROVERSY

(Emperor Leo III vs. John of Damascus)

ICONOCLASTIC CONTROVERSY (726-787)

When Leo III became emperor he issued a decree that images or pictures of

962 ◁ **886** ◁ **843** ◁ **830-950** ◁ **800** ◁ **726-787**

There was no cure and by the time it finished, over half the population of Europe had died.

WALES CONVERTED BY ST. DAVID; CHURCH BELLS USED IN FRANCE; CRUCIFIX BEGINNING TO BE USED IN CHURCHES

ST. COLUMBA FOUNDS MONASTERY ON IONA

MOHAMMED, FOUNDER OF ISLAM, IS BORN

POPE GREGORY THE GREAT

POPE GREGORY was made Pope in 590, even though he would have preferred to remain a monk. He is called the Great because he accomplished so much. He sent out missionaries to the Lombard tribes in Europe and to Britain to teach the people about Christianity. He wrote a manual for priests and bishops to teach them how to preach. He also introduced what became known as Gregorian chant, a new way of singing praises to God. He was the first pope to negotiate a treaty with a king.

FIRST CHURCH BELL IN ROME

BEGINNING OF ISLAM

ISLAM OFFICIALLY STARTED by Mohammed, an Arab living in Mecca. He started to see visions and hear voices around 610, and thought God was speaking to him. He said the voices told him to write the Qu'ran (Koran), which contained the true religion. However, it is a heresy because Islam denies that Jesus is God's Son.

| 542-594 | 550 | 563 | 570 | 590-604 | 604 | 622 |

Jesus should not be used in worship because they could only show Christ's humanity and not his divine nature. John of Damascus, a Syrian monk and priest, objected. He said the pictures were important because they reminded Christians that Christ was a real person. Both men said that images or pictures should not be worshipped.

BATTLE OF TOURS

BATTLE OF TOURS (732) Charles Martel, King of the Franks, defeated the Islamic army at the city of Tours. This was an important victory because it prevented the Muslims from moving any further in to Europe from the south.

ISLAM SPREAD FROM INDIA TO NORTH AFRICA AND INTO SPAIN

PSALMS TRANSLATED INTO ANGLO-SAXON; LINDISFARNE GOSPELS

FIRST MUSLIM SIEGE OF CONSTANT-INOPLE

MUSLIMS CAPTURE EGYPT, SYRIA AND MESAPOTAMIA; LIBRARY OF ALEXANDRIA DESTROYED

MUSLIMS CAPTURE JERUSALEM

ISLAMIC CAMPAIGNS (637-720) Beginning in 637 the Muslim nation began to expand its borders. Their army began by capturing Jerusalem and eventually spread out east to India and west through North Africa and into Spain. At first the conquering Muslims said that Jews and Christians were free to worship as they wanted to, but that quickly changed and persecution of Christians and Jews became common.

| 726-787 | 732 | 711-720 | 700 | 674 | 640-42 | 637 |

WHEN DID THE BISHOP OF ROME BECOME THE POPE?

In the 21st century the pope is the head of the Roman Catholic Church. But at the beginning of the church, there was no pope. Where did he come from? Who decided who should be pope?

In the Early Church, the Apostles were the church leaders. They taught the doctrines that Jesus had taught them to the small group of Christians. When the church began to grow, it was necessary to appoint more leaders to take care of each church in each city around the Roman world. The Apostles trained particular men to carry on leading the church after they died. And so it went on. Each generation of leaders, or bishops, trained the next generation to preach and teach the truth and prevent heresies from creeping into the church. No one bishop was more important than another. When there were difficulties in the church, the bishops would meet together in a council to discuss the problems and make decisions together.

The word 'pope' comes from the Latin word *papa* which means father. It was not unusual for early Christians to call their bishops Father. It was a title that meant respect. As people respected their own father in their family by obeying him, so they respected their 'father' in the church and obeyed his teachings.

No one woke up one day and suddenly decided to call the Bishop of Rome the Pope. It happened gradually, and the church found itself with a pope almost before they realised how it had happened. At the Council of Sardica in the middle of the 4th century, the bishops decided to give the Bishop of Rome the right to make final judgements on doctrinal disputes that a council could not settle. It was a 'just in case' clause, not something that should happen all the time. Unfortunately that's not what happened.

As time went on, the Bishop of Rome or pope as he was called at various times, began to get involved in politics. The city of Rome was invaded and vandalised, so popes became involved with rebuilding projects. Gregory the Great, who had no support from the emperor far away in Constantinople, had to rally the Roman soldiers himself to defend the city from yet more invaders.

In the middle of the 8th century Pepin, a Frankish nobleman, asked the pope to anoint him King of the Franks, which he did. This served to make an alliance between the king and the pope, meaning they could ask each other for help. By this time the pope had his own small army and owned a great deal of land throughout Western Europe. The land was donated by wealthy people over the years in order to get in good standing with the pope. Land had also been taken from people who were imprisoned or executed for various reasons. By the middle of the Medieval Age, the pope was not only the leader of the Western Church, but a politician, a military leader and landowner; a very powerful position.

Even though the pope's job had changed so much over the years, it didn't mean that they didn't care about the church. Some popes were very concerned about the spiritual welfare of the people. Others, sadly, were not.

WHAT IS ISLAM?

Islam is an Arabic word meaning 'submission to God.' Someone who follows the teachings of Islam is called a Muslim, which means 'one who submits.'

Where did the Islamic religion come from? It started with one man called Mohammed, who lived in the city of Mecca in the 7th century. Mohammed was raised by his uncle and when he grew up, he became a trader, someone who buys and sells goods, often traveling about.

Mohammed married and had five children. When Mohammed travelled, he would often stop for a while in a cave outside Mecca where he would meditate. When he was about forty years old, he began to hear voices and see visions and he thought they came from God. At some point he said he was given words to write down that became known as the Qur'an or Koran, which is Arabic for 'the recitation' (something repeated out loud from memory).

Mohammed believed that these words came from an angel of God.

At first very few believed Mohammed or wanted to read his book. People laughed at him and persecuted his followers. In 622 Mohammed and his followers ran away to the city of Medina and this is considered the beginning of the Islamic religion. Over time more and more Arabic people began to believe that Islam was the only true religion and Mohammed was God's prophet.

In 632 Mohammed returned to Mecca on a pilgrimage to kiss the black stone at the Kaaba, which has become something every Muslim should do once in their lifetime.

WHAT DO MUSLIMS AND CHRISTIANS BELIEVE?

	GOD	SALVATION	PROPHETS	GOD'S WORD
MUSLIMS	There is only one God, who is called Allah.	Everyone has a choice: worship Allah and obey his will or follow your own desires. Allah will only guide those who choose him.	There have been three major prophets from Allah: Moses, Jesus and Mohammed	The Qur'an contains the holy words of Allah
CHRISTIANS	There is only one true and living God. There are three persons in the one God, the Father, the Son, and the Holy Spirit. This is called the Trinity.	We are dead in our sins and unable to save ourselves. God sent his Son to die in our place to take away our sin and give us eternal life.	God sent many prophets to speak to his people in Israel in the Old Testament. Moses was a great prophet. Jesus was much more than a prophet. He was God's Son and not just another human being. Mohammed was not God's prophet.	Only the Bible contains the Word of God

After Mohammed's death, a new caliph (leader) was appointed to rule, both in religion and the state. Then Muslims began to expand their territory into Syria, Lebanon, Jordan and especially Palestine, because Muslims believed they had a holy right to Jerusalem. This belief was based on a dream that Mohammed had shortly before he died, where he was taken by an angel to Jerusalem and told to claim it for Allah.

The Muslim expansion led to many wars over the centuries as they conquered countries from India, through North Africa and into Spain. The people of every country or tribe they conquered were urged to become Muslims. Everyone who chose not to convert was treated harshly and prevented from worshipping openly.

CHURCH DIVIDED INTO EAST AND WEST

CHURCH DIVIDED INTO EAST AND WEST: In 1054 bishops from Rome went to Constantinople to discuss their differences about the Nicene Creed among other issues. The meeting did not go well. Neither side listened to the other and people lost their tempers. By the end, each side (Western and Eastern) excommunicated each other and refused to have anything to do with the other.

BATTLE OF HASTINGS

POPE GREGORY VII EXCOMMUN-ICATES EMPEROR HENRY IV

MUSLIMS BEGIN TO KEEP CHRISTIANS FROM MAKING PILGRIMAGES TO THE HOLY LAND

PILGRIMAGES: During the Middle Ages people would often make a journey to the Holy Land (Israel) to see the places where Jesus lived and died and rose again. They hoped this would bring them closer to God, and sometimes they would have special prayer requests such as asking for healing or guidance. Traveling was dangerous because of thieves and persecution from the Muslims who ruled the Middle East.

FIRST UNIVERSITY FOUNDED IN BOLOGNA, ITALY

BERNARD OF CLAIRVAUX

1054	1066	1073	1079	1088	1093-1153

FALL OF ACRE

FALL OF ACRE The city of Acre was the last stronghold that the Crusaders held in the Kingdom of Jerusalem. When the Turkish army finally captured it in 1291, the land of Palestine became part of the Ottoman Empire, and the crusades were essentially finished. Other future crusades never succeeded in regaining any part of Palestine.

SECOND COUNCIL OF LYONS

SECOND COUNCIL OF LYONS (1274) wrote out the doctrine of purgatory. Purgatory, said the church leaders, was the place Christians went to after they died and before they went to heaven, to finally cleanse them from sins they had committed. This doctrine was later rejected by the Reformers.

THOMAS AQUINAS WRITES SUMMA THEOLOGICA

THOMAS AQUINAS (1225-1274) was an Italian Dominican friar and priest who was known as a philosopher and theologian. He wrote Summa Theologica, which was an organised explanation of Christian doctrines. It continues to be studied today.

FIFTH, SIXTH AND SEVENTH CRUSADES

DOMINICAN ORDER OF PREACHERS ESTABLISHED

DOMINICAN ORDER OF PREACHERS was founded by a Spanish priest Dominic de Guzman. Members of the order were called friars

1291	1274	1265-1274	1219-1248	1216

BERNARD OF CLAIRVAUX

BERNARD OF CLAIRVAUX (1093-1153) was a French monk who became an abbot and formed a monastery at Clairvaux. He was a gifted preacher, theologian and writer, who became an advisor and negotiator for the pope and several kings. At the pope's command, Bernard successfully used his preaching to urge men to join in the Second Crusade against the Muslims.

FIRST CRUSADE

FIRST USE OF STAINED GLASS (ST. DENIS ABBEY IN PARIS)

SECOND CRUSADE

PETER LOMBARD WRITES FOUR BOOKS OF SENTENCES

PETER LOMBARD (1100-1160) was a theologian and professor at Notre Dame University in Paris in the mid-12th century. He wrote *The Four Books of Sentences*, the first systematic (or organised system) theology textbook, which became a standard university text. These very long books explained the Trinity, Creation and the Fall, Jesus' redeeming work, the sacraments and the final judgement.

PETER WALDO CONVERTED, FOUNDS THE WALDENSIAN PROTESTANT CHURCH

WALDENSIAN PROTESTANT CHURCH was started in France in the late 12th century by Peter Waldo, a wealthy merchant who gave away all his property to preach. Waldensians taught that the Bible was the sole rule of life and faith and rejected the authority of the pope and teachings about purgatory, indulgences and the mass. Pope Lucius III declared them heretics in 1184 because they rejected his authority.

1093-1153 ▸ **1096-99** ┈ **1135** ┈ **1147-48** ┈ **1150** ┈ **1174**

and were to travel around preaching the Gospel, educating ordinary people about the Bible in their own language.

MAGNA CARTA SIGNED BY KING JOHN AND THE ENGLISH NOBLES

FOURTH LATERAN COUNCIL

FOURTH CRUSADE FINISHES WITH THE LOOTING OF CONSTANTINOPLE

CRUSADES There were seven crusades, or battle campaigns in all. European Christians were urged by various popes to form an army to defeat the Muslims who had taken over Palestine. The Muslims were preventing Christians from visiting Jerusalem and other sites where Jesus had lived, and they were also persecuting any who would not convert to Islam.

THIRD CRUSADE

WALDENSIANS DECLARED HERETICS BY POPE LUCIUS III

FRANCIS OF ASSISI

FRANCIS OF ASSISI (1182-1226) was a hermit and then a traveling preacher. He founded the First Order of Franciscans, who became known as friars. They renounced possessions and travelled around Europe preaching the Gospel. He also founded the Order of Poor Clares for women who wished to dedicate their lives to God.

◂ **1216** ◂ **1215** ◂ **1215** ◂ **1200-04** ◂ **1189-92** ◂ **1184** ◂ **1182-1226**

TWO CHURCHES: EAST & WEST

The separation of churches goes back to Constantine in the 4th century when the empire was split into east and west. There were two capital cities: Rome (west) and Constantinople (east). These two parts of the empire sometimes worked together and sometimes not. And like the empire the church also separated into a western and eastern part. Both churches still worshipped God but developed some differences. In the western part of the church the worship services and religious books were all written in Latin, the language most people spoke there. In the eastern part the worship services and books were in Greek, the most common language there.

As time went on, other things became different too. In the west the role of the Bishop of Rome began to change from one among many bishops to becoming the most important bishop, and he was called the Pope. In the Eastern Church the bishop who lived in Constantinople was called the Patriarch, but he did not become the most important bishop, although he was the bishop who advised the emperor. Instead he met with other eastern bishops in councils to discuss doctrinal issues and any other problems that needed attention.

There were sparks between the two churches over the centuries. The debate about using images in worship (Iconoclastic controversy between those who rejected icons and others like John of Damascus who accepted them) caused a lot of hard feeling in the 8th century. In the following century there was conflict between Pope Nicolas I and Patriarch Photius over whether Christians living in what we now call the Balkans were part of the Western or the Eastern Church.

A debate over a doctrinal issue also arose. Both churches agreed with the Nicene Creed that was written in 325. However, around the 6th century the Western Church added a few words in the final paragraph about the Holy Spirit that the Eastern Church thought were wrong.

'We believe in the Holy Spirit, the Lord and giver of life, who proceeds from the Father and the Son'

The original phrase did not have the words 'and the Son.' The Eastern Church believed that adding the phrase 'and the Son' made the Holy Spirit a less important person in the Trinity. The Western Church insisted that was not what the phrase meant. Since both sides were already arguing about other issues, they would not listen to each other.

In 1053 the Western Church sent a delegation to try and patch up the relationship between east and west. However, the delegation came with a list of things that they demanded the Eastern Church agree to. Not a good way to begin, especially when the list began with: the pope shall be recognised as the head of the church. The Eastern Church responded with: only Christ is the head of the church. After that all the other issues such as the question of the correct version of the Nicene Creed, rules on fasting, what type of bread could be used in the Lord's Supper, and should priests be allowed to marry were just more things to argue about. Sadly the men at the meeting lost their tempers and said that the others were not Christians and should be excommunicated.

The excommunications were revoked a short time later after the men on both sides had died, but the hard feelings remained. Some attempts to talk to each other were made, but that came to a complete halt in 1204 when the Fourth Crusade destroyed the city of Constantinople. The two churches remain apart today.

THE CRUSADES: WHAT WERE THEY FIGHTING FOR?

The Crusades were a series of nine military campaigns in the years from 1096 to 1487. They began as a way to help the Byzantine Empire, which was being threatened by the Muslim Turkish armies and to rescue the Holy Land (Israel and Palestine today) from Muslim control.

Byzantine Emperor Alexios I sent an urgent plea to Pope Urban II asking him to send him an army to help hold off the invading Turks in 1095. The request wasn't just a military one. The Eastern Church was being persecuted, and they needed the Western Church to help. In addition, both churches were very concerned that pilgrims who travelled to the Holy Land were now persecuted and sometimes killed by Muslims as well as bandits. So Pope Urban gave a rousing speech, calling Christian knights to ready themselves for battle. The pope said that those who went on this crusade would have their sins forgiven. Here's what he meant by that: Every time a knight went into any battle, he had to kill the enemy, which was breaking the sixth commandment. So after any battle the knight would go to church and confess his sin and receive absolution (forgiveness) from the priest. Pope Urban was telling the knights that they would receive forgiveness for killing during the crusade because they were doing the right thing. Many knights joined up right away, even whole families of sons along with their fathers. It was an expensive journey. They had to provide all their own equipment, food, horses and servants, but in their eyes it was worth it, if they were helping God's people and would be forgiven for killing in battle.

The first crusade was successful. They captured Jerusalem and drove the Muslim army back from Palestine and the borders of the Byzantine Empire. The hard work done, many of the knights turned around and went home, but some stayed because someone had to govern the land. Palestine was divided into four kingdoms and ruled until 1130 when the Muslims began to fight back again. And so began an extended time when more crusades were necessary.

However, none were as successful as the first. The Muslim forces won the second one in 1154. In 1189 King Richard (known as the Lionheart) and the King of France led the third crusade.

The route taken by the crusaders

That one ended in 1192 with a peace treaty between Richard and Saladin, the Muslim general.

More crusades were fought but by the last one in 1487, little had been achieved. Many people died trying to free the Holy Land for Christians to live in or to safely travel on pilgrimage. Those willing to help fund the cost of the armies stopped giving their money. Added to this, not everyone who participated in the various crusades behaved well. The worst event was the destruction of Constantinople in 1204 by crusaders. The crusaders and the people of Constantinople were supposed to be on the same side, fighting against the Muslims. Instead, the crusaders became greedy for money and the beautiful things that the people of Constantinople had, and they ransacked the eastern city. This and other bad behaviour have given the Crusades a bad name, distracting people from any good that was accomplished.

TIMELINE: LATE MIDDLE AGES 1300-1500

'BABYLONIAN CAPTIVITY' OF THE PAPACY, WHICH MOVES TO AVIGNON

'BABYLONIAN CAPTIVITY' OF THE PAPACY (1309-1377) A long dispute began between Pope Boniface VIII and King Philip IV of France over who had the greater power: the pope or the king. After Boniface died, Philip made sure that the next elected pope was French and had the papal court moved to Avignon, where the next seven popes lived instead of in Rome. Finally Pope Gregory XI moved the papal court back to Rome in 1377. Sadly the papacy was becoming more concerned about political matters than spiritual ones.

GREAT FAMINE IN EUROPE

RAMON LULL, FIRST MISSIONARY TO THE MUSLIMS, STONED TO DEATH

RAMON LULL (CA.1235-1316) was the first missionary to the Muslims. Born in Spain, Ramon was converted when he was thirty years old. He studied the Arabic language so he could witness to the Muslims. He travelled to North Africa three times as a missionary. During his final visit, when he was eighty years old, he was stoned and later died of his injuries.

HUNDRED YEARS' WAR

1346-53 BLACK DEATH SPREADS FROM ASIA TO EUROPE, THE MIDDLE EAST AND NORTH AFRICA

BLACK DEATH was a terrible disease that began in the 1330s in China. It received its name from the black spots that appeared on the

1309 **1315-17** **1316** **1337** **1346-53**

ERASMUS ORDAINED

ERASMUS OF ROTTERDAM (1466-1536) was a Dutch theologian, teacher, and priest. He was critical of the abuses in the church, but remained a strong supporter of the pope. He used the best Greek manuscripts of the New Testament for his Latin translation, which helped those who later translated the Bible into their national languages during and after the Reformation.

MARTIN LUTHER BORN

THE BIBLE IS THE FIRST BOOK PRINTED ON THE PRINTING PRESS

MUSLIMS CAPTURE CONSTANTINOPLE; END OF THE EASTERN ROMAN EMPIRE

JOHANNES GUTENBERG INVENTS THE PRINTING PRESS

GUTENBERG PRINTING PRESS, JOHANNES GUTENBERG (CA.1398-1468), a German goldsmith, came up with the idea

1492 **1483** **1454** **1453** **1440**

skin. People could die from the disease in less than a day. The disease arrived in Italy in 1347 and quickly spread through all of Europe, killing 25 million people in five years. Animals died from it too. So many sheep died during that time that there was a wool shortage in Europe.

Many people were so afraid of catching the plague that they abandoned their sick friends and relatives.

JAN HUS

JAN HUS (CA.1369-1415) Born in Bohemia, Jan was educated in Prague, where he became a university professor and a priest and was appointed preacher at Bethlehem Chapel. Influenced by the teachings of John Wycliffe, Jan began calling for reform in the church. He criticised the church leaders who led immoral lives and he encouraged his students and congregation to read the Bible for themselves, rather than relying on church leaders to tell them what to believe about God.

PAPAL COURT MOVES BACK TO ROME

THE GREAT SCHISM

THE GREAT SCHISM (1378-1417) began the year after the papal court returned to Rome from Avignon. Not everyone agreed that the pope should have returned to Rome. The cardinals (church leaders) in Avignon elected a French pope, while the cardinals in Rome elected their own pope. The popes in Avignon were called the antipopes, while the pope in Rome was considered the real head of the western church. This messy situation lasted for thirty-nine years.

1346-53 • **1369-1415** • **1377** • **1378-1417**

---

of moveable type, or metal letters that could be arranged in any desired order to form words and sentences. This meant the type or letters could be used over and over again and made the printing press a practical possibility. In 1454 Johannes began to print the Bible. He printed 200 copies and sold them at the Frankfurt Book Fair in 1455. Fifty copies still exist today.

JOAN OF ARC WINS BATTLE OF ORLEANS

COUNCIL OF CONSTANCE

COUNCIL OF CONSTANCE (1414-1418) is known for two things: solving the Great Schism and condemning John Wycliffe and Jan Hus. Bishops, cardinals, kings and representatives from the universities gathered to solve the matter of too many popes. By this time three men were claiming to be the true pope. Finally one man was chosen, Pope Martin V. The Council also labelled Wycliffe and Hus as heretics.

Wycliffe was already dead, so they dug up his bones and burned them. Jan Hus was burned at the stake.

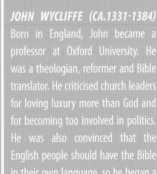

WYCLIFFE BEGINS TO TRANSLATE THE BIBLE INTO ENGLISH

JOHN WYCLIFFE (CA.1331-1384) Born in England, John became a professor at Oxford University. He was a theologian, reformer and Bible translator. He criticised church leaders for loving luxury more than God and for becoming too involved in politics. He was also convinced that the English people should have the Bible in their own language, so he began a translation project that was carried on by his students after his death.

1440 ◄ **1429** ◄ **1415** ◄ **1381**

REFORMING CHURCH

THE REFORMATION: HOW IT ALL BEGAN

he Reformation caused a huge change in all of Western society. Before the Reformation, everyone in the west went to the same church, called the Catholic (universal) church. After the Reformation there were two churches in the west: the Protestant Church (protesting against the Catholic Church) and the remaining Roman Catholic Church. It didn't happen all in one year. Instead there were a series of events in different countries that led to the entire period being called the Reformation.

The man who started it all was Martin Luther, who lived in the German state of Saxony. Martin's father wanted him to be a lawyer. However, Martin's life took a very different turn. One night as he was travelling home from university, a terrible thunderstorm began. Martin was out in the open with no place to take shelter while the lightning was striking all around him. He was very frightened and he began to pray very hard, asking God to protect him. He even bargained with God: if God would keep him safe through the storm, Martin would give up his law studies and become a monk. Martin survived the storm and kept his promise to God, even though it angered his father.

Martin joined the Augustinian Friars monastery. Soon the abbot realised that Martin was very bright and should continue his university studies, but this time in theology. After he had finished, Martin became a university professor and was ordained as a priest. However, even though he had all that knowledge in his head, Martin didn't understand the Gospel. He thought he had to work as hard as he could to please God and only then would God forgive his sins. But it did not work. Martin knew he was still sinful. Then one day, while he was preparing his lecture on Romans for his students, God suddenly gave Martin clear understanding. He read, 'The righteous shall live by faith'. Faith in Jesus Christ, not the works of Martin Luther, brought salvation! From that day, Martin knew God's peace in his soul, and now he could teach his students and his congregation the true Gospel.

The next year Martin heard a disturbing rumour. The pope had sent Johann Tetzel, a Dominican Friar, to the towns and villages to raise money for the church. Friar Tetzel was selling indulgences, pieces of paper that told people their sins were forgiven, as well as the sins of their loved ones in purgatory. Many people believed Tetzel and bought the indulgences. But when Martin heard about it, he was angry that so many people were being fooled about God's salvation. So he sat down and wrote out all the reasons why selling indulgences was wrong. He ended up writing 95 theses, or reasons, and he nailed the list to the church door, where everyone could read it. He also sent a copy to the church leaders, and eventually the pope himself received a copy.

Pope Leo was not pleased to receive criticism from an unknown priest and university professor, although Martin was surprised that the Pope and other church leaders were so angry with him. He had thought they just needed to be reminded of what God's Word taught and they would stop the selling of indulgences. Instead, they told Martin he was wrong and eventually put him on trial for heresy and excommunicated him. However, the Duke of Saxony sent soldiers to rescue Martin and hid him in a castle for a year. During that time Martin translated the New Testament into German, so people could read God's Word for themselves. Then the Duke of Saxony invited Martin to live and teach in Wittenberg once more, where the Duke could protect him from the pope.

Martin Luther's actions officially began the Protestant Reformation. He protested against the wrong teaching of the Catholic Church leaders, and the split in the western church became official.

TIMELINE: REFORMING CHURCH 1500-1530

PRINTING PRESSES IN EUROPE PUBLISHING 1,000 BOOKS PER YEAR

LUTHER ENTERS THE AUGUSTINIAN MONASTERY IN ERFURT

LUTHER ORDAINED

FRIAR TETZEL ARRIVES IN GERMANY TO SELL INDULGENCES

SELLING INDULGENCES was the practice of selling a piece of paper that said peoples' sins were forgiven. The reasoning went like this: people were required to come to their priest to confess their sins and then be told that God forgave them. People were also supposed to give offerings to the church. So why not combine them: tell people that their sins were forgiven by giving them a piece of paper when the people gave money to the church. They could also buy forgiveness for their loved ones in purgatory. Then it was taken further. Friar Tetzel, when he came to sell indulgences in Germany, didn't bother with people confessing their sins. He just wanted them to pay the money.

LUTHER POSTS HIS 95 THESES AT WITTENBERG

1500-40 ▸ **1505** ▸ **1507** ▸ **1516** ▸ **1517** ▸

AUGSBURG CONFESSION

AUGSBURG CONFESSION (1530) is the primary confession of faith of the Lutheran Church. It consists of 28 articles on what Lutherans believe about God, salvation, the sacraments, church order and how a Christian should behave. It was written by Philip Melanchthon, a friend of Martin Luther.

MARBURG COLLOQUY

MARBURG COLLOQUY (1529) was a meeting that took place at Marburg Castle in Germany. Martin Luther and Ulrich Zwingli met to discuss what they disagreed about the Lord's Supper. Luther said the Christ was Present in the elements of the wine and bread. Zwingli said the wine and bread were only symbols. After four days they stopped the discussion because they could not agree.

SWISS CANTONS (STATES) ARE DIVIDED BETWEEN REFORMED AND ROMAN CATHOLIC

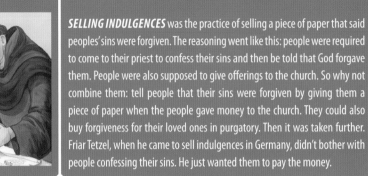

THOSE WHO BROKE AWAY FROM ROME ARE NOW CALLED PROTESTANTS

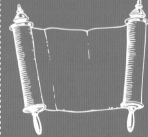

◂ **1530** ◂ **1529** ◂ **1529** ◂ **1529**

LUTHER PUBLISHES ON THE FREEDOM OF A CHRISTIAN

LUTHER'S ON THE FREEDOM OF A CHRISTIAN (1520) was an important book. He told Christians that they could not earn their salvation through good works. Their salvation came through faith in Jesus Christ alone. He also told them that the Bible was the final authority from God, not the pope.

LUTHER EXCOMMUNICATED

LUTHER TRANSLATES THE NEW TESTAMENT INTO GERMAN, ALONG WITH PAMPHLETS CRITICISING THE CHURCH

PEASANTS' REVOLT IN GERMANY

PEASANTS' REVOLT (1524-25) took place in the German-speaking states of the Holy Roman Empire. Peasants were angry about high taxes, unfair trials and serfdom. They also wanted the right to call or elect their own pastors. The peasants used the excuse that Luther had rebelled against the Roman Catholic Church to rebel against the nobility. Luther did not support the revolt and preached against it. Many thousands of people died before the revolt was stopped.

1517 **1520** **1521** **1522** **1524**

FIRST BAPTIST CHURCH ESTABLISHED IN ZURICH

LUTHER WRITES THE HYMN A MIGHTY FORTRESS IS OUR GOD

SWISS BRETHREN (ANABAPTISTS) FORMED IN ZURICH

ANABAPTISTS, OR SWISS BRETHREN, are Christians who believe in waiting to baptise a person until they make profession of faith. They believe that baptising infants is wrong and insist on re-baptising anyone who had been baptised as an infant. The Zurich council forced the group to leave the city when they would not change their opinion on baptism.

TYNDALE'S ENGLISH TRANSLATION OF THE NEW TESTAMENT PUBLISHED

TYNDALE'S NEW TESTAMENT William Tyndale, an English priest and professor, translated the New Testament into English. He had to do it secretly, hiding out in various cities in Europe because King Henry VIII had made it illegal to translate the Bible in England. Tyndale's New Testament was smuggled into England and distributed secretly.

1527 **1527** **1525** **1525**

WHAT HAPPENED NEXT

IN SWITZERLAND

In 1519 Ulrich Zwingli began teaching similar doctrines to Luther in Switzerland, and slowly the Swiss Reformed Church formed as another part of the Protestant church.

IN FRANCE

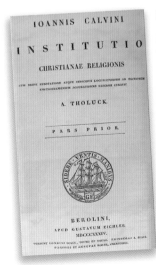

In 1536 Jean Calvin published a book called *The Institutes of the Christian Religion*. He wrote his book to help people understand the doctrines taught in God's Word, the Bible. The country of France remained Roman Catholic and King Francis had Protestants arrested and put in prison. Calvin fled to safety in Switzerland. In 1541 he was invited to pastor the church in Geneva, where he taught the doctrines he had written about in his book. Many fugitive Protestants, including John Knox, came to Geneva to be taught by Calvin.

IN ENGLAND

In 1534 King Henry VIII of England broke away from the Roman Catholic Church because the Pope refused to grant him a divorce from Queen Catherine. He declared himself the head of the church, and five years later had the English Bible placed in every church in the country. Two of King Henry's three children were Protestants. King Edward VI became king after his father and continued the reformation of the church. Queen Mary followed her brother, but since she was Roman Catholic, she tried to undo as much of the reformation as she could. After her five year reign came Queen Elizabeth I, who returned the country to the Protestant church, called the Church of England.

IN SCOTLAND

John Knox returned to Scotland in 1559, the year after the Protestant Princess Elizabeth became queen of England. He helped write the Scots Confession that abolished the Pope's authority in Scotland and laid out what the Scottish Church believed and taught. John Knox continued to teach and preach throughout Scotland, and is credited with forming the Presbyterian Church as another of the Protestant churches.

IN NORTHERN EUROPE

In Sweden King Gustav I made Lutheranism the national religion in 1523. Denmark remained officially Roman Catholic until 1536 when King Christian III declared the country Lutheran. However, no Protestant had been persecuted in Denmark since the 1530s. The Netherlands were ruled by the Spanish Roman Catholic King Philip II, who persecuted Protestants. However, the people chose to be Protestant and in the 1560s the Spanish were forced out and the Dutch Reformed Church was founded.

TRANSLATING THE BIBLE

The Bible was originally written in the Hebrew language (Old Testament) and the Greek language (New Testament) because those were the languages that people spoke at that time. However, as the Romans took over the known world, Latin became the common language of the people, and the Bible needed to be translated into Latin. Pope Damasus asked Jerome, a monk and well-known scholar, to begin translating the New Testament in 382 A.D. Twenty-three years later Jerome completed both the Old and New Testaments. This Latin Bible was called the Vulgate, which meant 'in the common language.'

For many years, only the Latin Bible was available even though the common language began to change as the Roman Empire began to break up. During this time of change and upheaval, few people were educated or could read so there was not a demand for the Bible in other languages. The priests and bishops learned Latin in order to read the Bible and then they would tell their congregations what it said.

During the Middle Ages some translations were made of various books of the Bible. Books, however, were expensive to make at that time because they were copied out by hand a page at a time by monks and nuns in the monasteries. So it was more common to have one book of the Bible or selections of Psalms and prayers in a book for wealthy people to buy. In the 14th century an English priest and scholar, John Wycliffe decided that the English people needed the entire Bible in their own language. He began his project with the help of his students at Oxford University, but he died before it was completed. Fortunately his students carried on and by 1396 the entire Bible had been translated into the common language of the people.

Translating God's Word wasn't just an interesting project for scholars. They knew that the Bible was the most powerful book in the world and that people needed to be able to read it. With the Bible more available, God began to stir people's hearts toward reforming the church. Church leaders had drifted away from teaching God's truth and became more interested in power and wealth. With the Reformation came the realisation that more translations were needed. All people, regardless of which language they spoke, needed God's Word. So God raised up men like Luther, William Tyndale and others to translate His Word into the common languages of their century.

William Tyndale, Bible Translator c. 1494 - 1536

TIMELINE: REFORMING CHURCH 1534-1546

LUTHER COMPLETES GERMAN TRANSLATION OF OLD TESTAMENT

ENGLAND BREAKS AWAY FROM THE ROMAN CATHOLIC CHURCH

COVERDALE BIBLE PUBLISHED, FIRST COMPLETE ENGLISH BIBLE

COVERDALE BIBLE (1535) Miles Coverdale used Tyndale's translation of the New Testament and the first five books of the Old Testament and then completed the translation of the rest of the Old Testament himself.

CALVIN PUBLISHES *THE INSTITUTES OF THE CHRISTIAN RELIGION*

INSTITUTES OF THE CHRISTIAN RELIGION
John Calvin, a lawyer, wrote *The Institutes* to educate people who were new to the Protestant faith. He explained the Law of God, the Apostles' Creed, the Lord's Prayer and the Sacraments of Baptism and the Lord's Supper. Calvin wrote all this in one volume, but as the years went on, he revised and added more explanations until the last edition in 1559 contained 80 chapters. This book is still read and studied today by many Christians.

1534 | **1534** | **1535** | **1536**

MARTIN LUTHER DIES

BORN
10 NOV 1483
DIED
18 FEB 1546
EISLEBEN

COUNCIL OF TRENT

COUNCIL OF TRENT was a series of meetings of Roman Catholic bishops in the towns of Trent and Bologna in Northern Italy. They met several times during an eighteen-year period. By the end of the meetings the Roman Catholic Church declared that only they could interpret Scripture properly, traditions of the church were just as important as the Bible, and all Protestants were heretics.

THE CONGREGATION OF THE INQUISITION ESTABLISHED

Galileo before the Holy Office

CONGREGATION OF THE INQUISITION was established by Pope Paul III to defend the Roman Catholic Faith, stop the spread of Protestantism and punish those who indulged in witchcraft and other wrong practices. Those suspected of heresy were arrested and tried in a church court; if found guilty, they could be sent to prison or executed.

CALVIN INVITED TO RETURN TO GENEVA TO PASTOR THE CHURCH

CALVIN AND GENEVA Calvin was first persuaded to become the pastor of the Genevan church by William Farel in 1536. Within two years the city councillors were angry with Calvin for refusing the Lord's Supper to people who misbehaved. Calvin and Farel were told to leave Geneva. After three years in Strasburg, Calvin received

1546 | **1545-1563** | **1542** | **1541**

WILLIAM TYNDALE SENTENCED TO DEATH

WILLIAM TYNDALE (1494-1536) hid from King Henry VIII's soldiers for 10 years before they finally caught him in the Netherlands. Tyndale was kept a prisoner for 18 months and then was sentenced to death by strangulation and burning.

HENRY VIII BEGINS DISSOLVING THE MONASTERIES

CALVIN BECOMES PASTOR IN GENEVA FOR THE FIRST TIME

DENMARK-NORWAY BECOME LUTHERAN

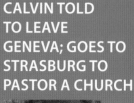

CALVIN TOLD TO LEAVE GENEVA; GOES TO STRASBURG TO PASTOR A CHURCH

1536 **1536** **1536** **1536** **1538**

an apology and invitation to return to Geneva, which he accepted. He remained as pastor there for the rest of his life. Geneva became the place where exiled Reformers came to study until it was safe for them to return to their own countries to teach the Gospel.

BRETHREN CHURCH IN THE NETHERLANDS NOW CALLED MENNONITES

MENNONITES are a Christian group belonging to the Anabaptist tradition. It was first formed in the Netherlands under the leadership of Menno Simons. He taught that Mennonites must remain separate from the world and not to participate in war.

SOCIETY OF JESUS (JESUITS) FORMED BY IGNATIUS LOYOLA AND SIX OTHERS

SOCIETY OF JESUS The Jesuits were formed in 1540 to serve the Roman Catholic Church by evangelising, caring for the poor, teaching children, establishing orphanages, schools and universities. They were also sent as missionaries to India, Africa, South and North America and the Far East.

HENRY VIII HAS ENGLISH BIBLE PLACED IN EVERY CHURCH

HENRY VIII HAD ENGLISH BIBLE PLACED IN EVERY CHURCH Just before William Tyndale died he prayed a short prayer: 'Lord, open the king of England's eyes.' God answered Tyndale's prayer three years later. King Henry changed the law that made English Bibles illegal, and allowed Coverdale's English Bible to be printed. He also ordered that an English Bible should be placed in every church in the country.

1541 **1540** **1540** **1539**

HOW THE ROMAN CATHOLIC CHURCH RESPONDED

The pope and other Roman Catholic Church leaders were very angry at those who had caused the Reformation, but they were also aware that some things within their Church did need to be fixed. As a result, Pope Paul III called for a council of bishops and cardinals to meet to discuss both doctrine (what the church should believe and teach) and behaviour of church leaders. It was a series of meetings that took place in the city of Trent beginning in 1545. Over the next eighteen years the council met three times and debated the doctrinal differences between the Protestants and the Roman Catholic Church. Here is what each side said was true.

The Council ended up deciding that the Protestants were wrong on all these doctrines and made no changes to what the Roman Catholic Church should teach. Instead they began to use their political power to arrest and kill Protestants.

Pope Pius V who became pope in 1566, did try to impose behavioural reforms in Rome. He was concerned that church leaders should live moral lives, according to the Bible, and not spend their time accumulating wealth. They should also be good teachers to their congregations.

DOCTRINAL ISSUE	PROTESTANTS	ROMAN CATHOLICS
SALVATION	Justification by faith	Faith plus obedience to the church and taking the sacraments
THE BIBLE	Bible is our only guide	Bible plus what the church has taught in the past (tradition)
SACRAMENTS	Two sacraments: Baptism and Lord's Supper	Seven sacraments: Baptism, Eucharist (Lord's Supper), Marriage, Confirmation, Reconciliation, Anointing the sick and dying, Holy Orders
APOCRYPHAL BOOKS	Not inspired by God	Part of inspired Word of God
MASS	Wrong because the words used say that Christ is sacrificed again and again	Necessary because Christ's sacrifice must be made for the people on an ongoing basis
LANGUAGE TO BE USED IN WORSHIP	Common language of the people	Always in the Latin language

SOLA
IS A LATIN WORD THAT MEANS 'ONLY'.

The Reformers came up with five easy ways to understand the Gospel.

SOLA SCRIPTURA	=	ONLY THE SCRIPTURES	The Bible is a Christian's only authority. It is God's Word and it contains all we need to know about God, salvation and how we should live.
SOLUS CHRISTUS	=	ONLY CHRIST	Salvation comes only through Jesus Christ, the Son of God. There is no other way to be saved.
SOLA GRATIA	=	ONLY GRACE	God has provided salvation for us even though we do not deserve it. He has chosen to provide it because he loves us.
SOLA FIDE	=	ONLY FAITH	God gives us the faith we need to believe in Jesus Christ. We can only be saved through faith. Nothing we try to do to please God will save us.
SOLI DEO GLORIA	=	ONLY FOR GOD'S GLORY	The reason for our salvation is to live a godly life that brings glory to God.

TIMELINE: REFORMING CHURCH 1547–1598

EDWARD VI, A PROTESTANT, BECOMES KING OF ENGLAND

THE BOOK OF COMMON PRAYER PUBLISHED

BOOK OF COMMON PRAYER (1549) was published during King Edward VI's reign as part of the Protestant English Reformation. Thomas Cranmer, Archbishop of Canterbury, oversaw the writing of the first English prayer book. It contained prayers for Sunday worship as well as special services like marriages and funerals, and readings from the Old and New Testaments for daily reading. The Book of Common Prayer was to teach both the clergy and the people how to worship in a Protestant church.

BIBLE TRANSLATED INTO DANISH

ICELAND BECOMES OFFICIALLY LUTHERAN

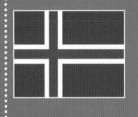

FIRST STATUTE OF REPEAL

THE FIRST STATUTE OF REPEAL QUEEN MARY I (1516-1558) was the oldest child of Henry VIII. She became queen after her brother, King Edward VI, died in 1553. She was Roman Catholic and had the First Statute of Repeal passed, which undid all the laws passed previously allowing the Protestant church. She became known as Bloody Mary because she had so many Protestants, including Thomas Cranmer, killed during her five-year reign.

1547 · **1549** · **1550** · **1550** · **1553**

EDICT OF NANTES

EDICT OF NANTES was a law passed by King Henry IV of France that gave some religious freedom to the Huguenots. They were allowed to worship publicly in certain areas and given access to education and fair treatment in the courts. However, they were limited as to where they could live. They could not settle in Paris or those parts of France that were officially Roman Catholic.

CHRISTIANITY BANNED IN JAPAN

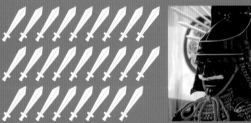
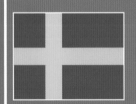

CHRISTIANITY BANNED IN JAPAN In 1549 Jesuit missionaries arrived in Japan and by 1582 over 200,000 people, including warlords, had converted to the Roman Catholic faith. In 1597 the most powerful warlord, Toyotomi Hideyoshi, had 26 Roman Catholic missionaries put to death and banned all forms of Christianity from Japan because he thought they were becoming too powerful.

SWEDEN BECOMES OFFICIALLY LUTHERAN

ST. BARTHOLOMEW'S DAY MASSACRE

ST. BARTHOLOMEW'S DAY MASSACRE (AUGUST 24, 1572) King Charles IX of France, a Roman Catholic, ordered his soldiers to kill all the French Protestants (known as Huguenots) who had gathered in Paris for his sister's wedding. The killing soon spread throughout France and over the next two months over 70,000 Huguenots were killed.

1598 · **1597** · **1593** · **1572**

THOMAS CRANMER EXECUTED FOR HERESY

INDEX OF PROHIBITED BOOKS ISSUED BY POPE PAUL IV

ELIZABETH I BECOMES QUEEN OF ENGLAND

ACT OF UNIFORMITY

Houses of Parliament today. Part of these buildings may have been built at that time of this Act but not all of them

ACT OF UNIFORMITY was a law passed by the English Parliament that required all churches in England to use the Book of Common Prayer. Queen Elizabeth wanted all churches to worship the same way in order to keep peace. However, the Puritans objected to being forced to use the Book of Common Prayer and other practices in worship such as kneeling to take the Lord's Supper.

GENEVA BIBLE PUBLISHED

GENEVA BIBLE William Whittingham, an Englishman, translated the Bible into English while he lived in Geneva during Mary I's reign. The Geneva Bible became very popular in the 16th and 17th centuries because it contained study notes and illustrations to help the reader understand the text better. It was also the first complete English Bible to be divided into chapters and verses.

1556   **1557**   **1558**   **1559**   **1560**

THIRTY-NINE ARTICLES FINALISED

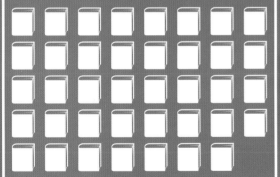

THIRTY-NINE ARTICLES was a statement of what the Church of England believed and how it was different from the Roman Catholic Church. It was written by Thomas Cranmer, Archbishop of Canterbury.

FOXE'S BOOK OF MARTYRS PUBLISHED

HEIDELBERG CATECHISM

HEIDELBERG CATECHISM (1562) was written by a group of Reformed ministers, in the city of Heidelberg, as a catechism to teach Reformed doctrine. It is divided into fifty-two sections, the same number of Lord's Days in a year, with the idea that people would spend time learning the confession as part of their Sunday activity.

SCOTS CONFESSION APPROVED BY SCOTTISH PARLIAMENT

SCOTS CONFESSION was the Confession of Faith written by six Scottish Protestant Reformers including John Knox, in just four days. Queen Mary I, a Roman Catholic, refused to sign it into law. The Regent, the Earl of Moray, approved it in 1567 and it became the Confession of the Church of Scotland.

1571   **1563**   **1562**   **1560**

PROTESTANT DENOMINATIONS

DENOMINATION:

A group of congregations that are united in what they believe and practice.

DENOMINATION	SALVATION	LORD'S SUPPER	BAPTISM	CHURCH GOVERNMENT
	✝	🍷🍞	🕊	🖋
REFORMED	All of God	Christ is spiritually present	Infant Baptism	Presbyterian
ANABAPTIST	Free will to resist or accept salvation	Memorial (remembering Jesus' death)	Adult or Believer's Baptism	Congregational
MENNONITE	Free will to resist or accept salvation	Memorial (remembering Jesus' death)	Adult or Believer's Baptism	Congregational
LUTHERAN	All of God	Christ is present in the bread and wine	Infant Baptism	Episcopal
ANGLICAN / EPISCOPAL	All of God	Christ is present in the bread and wine	Infant Baptism	Episcopal

PRESBYTERIAN:

Congregations are gathered into groups called Presbyteries, which oversee the congregations in their area. Each congregation is ruled or led by a group of elected elders called a session. The minister, elected by the congregation, is part of the session and answerable to the presbytery.

CONGREGATIONAL:

Each congregation rules itself, usually led by an elected board of elders or deacons. The pastor is elected by the congregation and answerable to them.

EPISCOPAL:

The church is governed by bishops. The archbishop appoints a bishop to oversee each diocese, which is made up of a group of congregations. The priest oversees the local congregation and is answerable to his bishop.

WHAT ABOUT THE QUAKERS?

Quakers believe that Jesus is the Son of God, but do not believe that we are sinful and need salvation. Instead they believe people are good and need to follow Jesus' teachings to live a life that pleases God. They do not practise Baptism or celebrate the Lord's Supper. Their meetings consist of silent meditation, waiting for God to speak to them.

We have already seen the hardships that the Eastern Church had suffered during the time of the crusades. Since the crusades could not stop the Muslims from continued warfare, they eventually captured all of what we call Turkey today, the Middle East and Northern Africa. By 1453 the city of Constantinople fell too.

The Eastern Church became a persecuted minority in the Muslim state. The Sultan did allow the Patriarch of the church to hold office, but only if the Patriarch paid a high fee to the Sultan and obeyed whatever the Sultan said. So it was difficult for the Patriarch to be a real leader to the church. Christians occasionally suffered physical persecution from government leaders, but they had other ways to make Christians' lives very uncomfortable.

All wealthy Christians had to give their money and land to the Sultan. Every Christian had to pay much higher taxes than their Muslim neighbours. Since Christians were so poor, the churches they were allowed to keep fell into ruin. Some of the churches were taken away from them and turned into mosques for Muslims to worship

WHAT ABOUT THE EASTERN CHURCH?

in, particularly the Hagia Sophia, the magnificent cathedral in the centre of Constantinople. Christians had to send their children to Muslim schools which taught the Islamic religion and trained children for the military. No Christian could hold any office in the government.

Russia was the only country in the east that was able to defend itself against the Muslim Turks. As a result the Eastern Church became split into two parts: the Greek Orthodox Church suffering under Muslim rule and the Russian Orthodox Church now centred in Moscow with its own Patriarch. In Russia the church had the support of the Tsar and the government. Some of the tax money went to support the church, and people could worship without fear of persecution. In 1589 the Russian Orthodox became independent of Constantinople.

TIMELINE: REFORMING CHURCH [PURITANS] 1603-1685

JAMES VI OF SCOTLAND BECOMES JAMES I OF ENGLAND

PURITANS were officially called Non-conformists during the reign of James I of England. As time went on all those who protested against the Church of England (Presbyterians, other Reformed churches, Baptists, and Congregationalist churches) were also called Non-conformists.

JACOB ARMINIUS DENIES PREDESTINATION = ARMINIANISM

ARMINIANISM was based on the teachings of Jacob Arminius, which state that God's grace is resistible and that man can make the conscious choice to be saved.

JOHN SMYTH ESTABLISHES THE BAPTIST CHURCH

KING JAMES VERSION OF THE BIBLE PUBLISHED

SYNOD OF DORT

SYNOD OF DORT was held to settle the controversy between Arminianism and Reformed teaching. Pastors and elders from several European countries discussed the two opinions and decided that the Reformed teaching was the biblical one. They also listed the five points of Calvinism, which are: **T**otal depravity, **U**nconditional election, **L**imited atonement, **I**rresistible grace, **P**erseverance of the saints.

1603 **1603** **1609** **1611** **1618**

EDICT OF NANTES REVOKED

EDICT OF NANTES was revoked by King Louis XIV of France causing mass exodus of Huguenots from France. Up until this time the Edict of Nantes had protected French Protestants from persecution. Many Huguenots fled to the Netherlands, the German states and Britain, while some went further to the New World colonies.

BUNYAN'S PILGRIM'S PROGRESS PUBLISHED

PIETISM BEGUN BY PHILIPP JAKOB SPENER

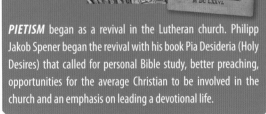

PIETISM began as a revival in the Lutheran church. Philipp Jakob Spener began the revival with his book Pia Desideria (Holy Desires) that called for personal Bible study, better preaching, opportunities for the average Christian to be involved in the church and an emphasis on leading a devotional life.

MILTON'S PARADISE LOST PUBLISHED

ACT OF UNIFORMITY

ACT OF UNIFORMITY (1662) made the use of The Book of Common Prayer compulsory in worship services in Britain. When a clergyman refused to use The Book of Common Prayer, he had to resign from pastoring his church. Over 2,000 Non-conformists lost their churches.

1685 **1678** **1675** **1667** **1662**

THIRTY YEARS WAR

BRITAIN BEGINS SLAVE TRADE FROM AFRICA TO JAMESTOWN VA

PILGRIMS LAND AT PLYMOUTH

PILGRIMS LAND IN PLYMOUTH a group of Puritans or Nonconformists left England on the Mayflower in order to set up a colony in the New World. They wanted religious freedom, which they were denied in England.

FIRST BAPTIST CHURCH FOUNDED IN RHODE ISLAND

CIVIL WAR IN ENGLAND

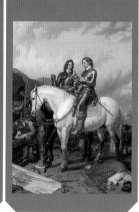

1618-1648   **1618**   **1620**   **1639**   **1642**

SEDITION ACT

SEDITION ACT (1661) revoked the Solemn League and Covenant. Charles II wanted England to return to the Anglican Church and *The Book of Common Prayer*. He imposed the Act of Uniformity on all Britain a year later.

GEORGE FOXE FOUNDED THE SOCIETY OF FRIENDS [QUAKERS]

WESTMINSTER CONFESSION OF FAITH

WESTMINSTER CONFESSION OF FAITH (1646) was drawn up by the Westminster Assembly as a Presbyterian confession of faith.

SOLEMN LEAGUE AND COVENANT

SOLEMN LEAGUE AND COVENANT (1643) was an agreement between the Scottish Covenanters and the leaders of the English Parliamentarians during the First English Civil War. The Scots agreed to supply troops to help defeat the Royalists, and the English agreed to unite their two churches and become Presbyterian.

1661   **1647**   **1646**   **1643**

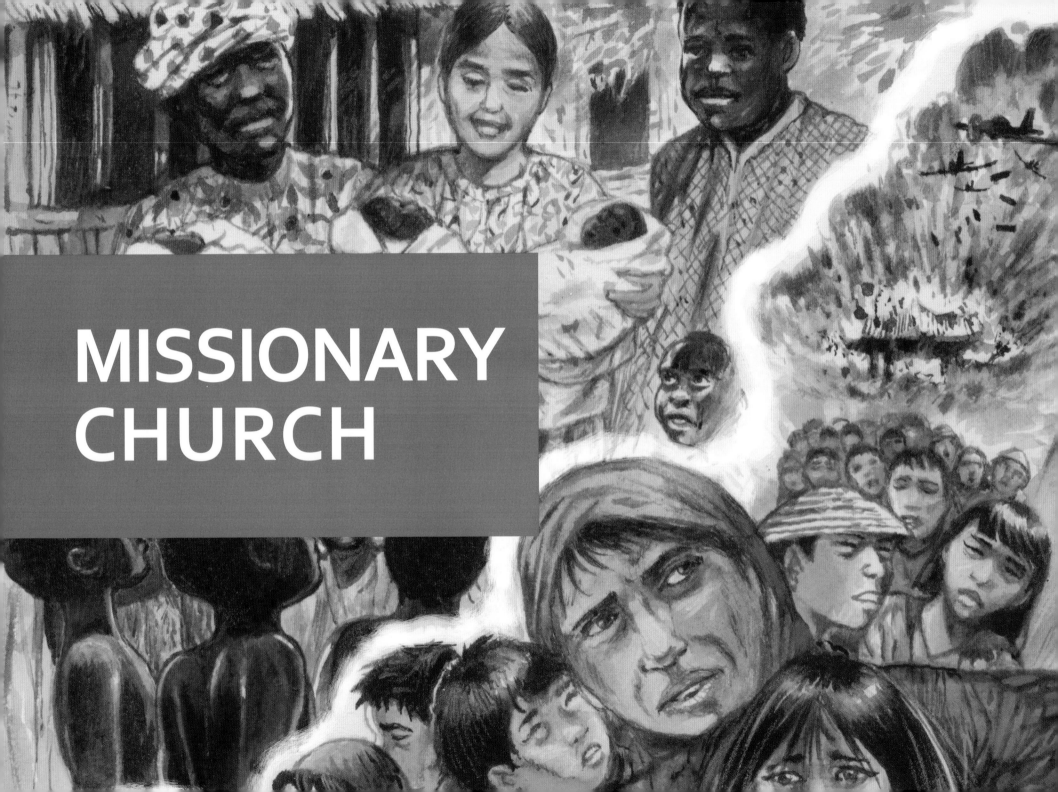

MISSIONARY CHURCH

GOD'S WONDER OF THE AGE

When George Whitfield was growing up in Gloucester, England, his dearest wish was to be an actor. He often skipped school to practise for his schoolboy performances. His mother wanted him to go to Oxford University but his parents didn't have the money for the tuition. So George paid for his own education by working at the university as a servitor. He waited on wealthy students by taking care of their clothes, bringing them meals and even helping them with their assignments. In between seventeen-year-old George attended classes.

George became interested in reading the Bible when he was fifteen, but it wasn't until he met John and Charles Wesley that he began to realise he needed 'the new birth.' He decided to join the Wesleys' 'Holy Club,' which was a group of university students eager to explore the Bible and live to please God. During that time, George experienced a conversion or what John Wesley called 'the new birth.' George was ready to dedicate his life to serving God. The following year in 1736, George was ordained a minister in the Church of England.

George's training in the theatre helped to make him a good preacher. He had learned how to project, or make his voice louder, so that even in crowds of 20,000 people, everyone could hear him. And many crowds that size often gathered in outdoor places to hear George present the Gospel. When he preached, no one stirred or made a noise. Even people who didn't want to know about God came to hear him because of his gift of oratory, and they got the Gospel too.

George, however, didn't think that God was calling him to a single church to pastor. Instead he was called to evangelise, which meant he travelled from place to place preaching, always preaching. On horseback or in a carriage, George travelled up and down England and Wales many times, preaching every day. He visited Scotland fourteen times and Ireland twice. Then he turned his sights on the American colonies, which he visited seven times. Visiting all thirteen colonies, he travelled over 1100 miles (approximately 1770 km) over dirt roads, going through forests and taking canoes along the coastline if there were no roads. For thirty-four years George preached the gospel until he literally wore out his body. Doctors told him to slow down, but he said: 'I would rather wear out than rust out.'

God used George to bring many people to faith and influence others to serve God. Jonathan Edwards, after hearing George preach, was encouraged to keep preaching to his congregation. Very soon afterwards the First Awakening began. William Wilberforce heard George Whitfield preach when he was a boy. As an adult, Wilberforce helped to have slavery banned in the British Empire. Many other people were also converted who then went on to be missionaries to many countries.

TIMELINE: MISSIONARY CHURCH 1700-1799

QUAKERS LEAVE ENGLAND TO SETTLE IN PENNSYLVANIA COLONY

SOCIETY FOR THE PROPAGATION OF THE GOSPEL IN FOREIGN PARTS ESTABLISHED

SOCIETY FOR THE PROPAGATION OF THE GOSPEL IN FOREIGN PARTS (1701) was established by the Church of England to send out missionaries and literature to the colonies of the British Empire. They also sponsored schools and teachers.

ISAAC WATTS PUBLISHES HIS *HYMNS AND SPIRITUAL SONGS* HYMNAL

PETER THE GREAT IMPOSES STATE CONTROL ON THE RUSSIAN ORTHODOX CHURCH

GREAT AWAKENING BEGINS IN AMERICAN COLONIES

GREAT AWAKENING IN THE AMERICAN COLONIES (1730) began with Jonathan Edwards, a Puritan minister in Massachusetts. Through his preaching, a revival began first in his church and then spread throughout the American colonies. Many people were converted and Christians were 'awakened' to serve God more faithfully.

1700 · · · **1701** · · · **1707** · · · **1721** · · · **1730**

CHURCH MISSIONARY SOCIETY OF THE CHURCH OF ENGLAND

NETHERLANDS MISSIONARY SOCIETY FOUNDED

SCOTTISH MISSIONARY SOCIETY FOUNDED

NEW YORK MISSIONARY SOCIETY FOUNDED

The City of New York in the 1700s

MISSIONARY SOCIETIES began to be formed as a result of the Second Great Awakening. While missionaries had been going out to other lands since the Early Church, these societies helped to provide more organisations to raise funds and supply regular support for the missionaries they sent out.

LONDON MISSIONARY SOCIETY FOUNDED

WILLIAM CAREY, FIRST BRITISH MISSIONARY, BEGINS HIS MISSION TO INDIA

1798 · **1797** · **1796** · **1796** · **1795** · **1793**

MORAVIAN MISSIONARIES ARE SENT OUT TO VARIOUS PARTS OF THE WORLD

GEORGE WHITFIELD AND JOHN WESLEY PREACH THE FIRST EVANGELISTIC OPEN-AIR SERMONS IN ENGLAND

WHITFIELD AND WESLEY had been prevented from preaching in Anglican churches because they had criticised some Anglican ministers for not preaching the Gospel clearly. So they set up in open fields and preached to people as they gathered there. George Whitfield was especially good at projecting his voice so that everyone in the huge crowds could hear him.

GEORGE FREDRICK HANDEL COMPOSES THE MESSIAH

METHODIST CHURCH FORMED

AGE OF ENLIGHTENMENT TAKES HOLD IN EUROPEAN SOCIETY

AGE OF ENLIGHTENMENT was a time when people's thoughts about science, philosophy, society and politics began to change. People began to think scientific reasoning was more important than what the church taught or obeying the government. This way of thinking led to revolutions in some countries.

1732 ▶ **1739** ▶ **1741** **1744** ▶ **1750** ▶

SECOND GREAT AWAKENING BEGINS IN AMERICA

FRENCH REVOLUTION

FRENCH REVOLUTION was a revolution against the French monarchy and the Roman Catholic Church, which lasted ten years. After it was over, the Roman Catholic Church could no longer participate in the French government.

AMERICAN DECLARATION OF INDEPENDENCE

AMERICAN DECLARATION OF INDEPENDENCE was a document signed by the American colonies at the end of their revolutionary war against Britain. They declared themselves no longer colonies, but one country free to rule itself. As part of the American constitution (1787) the church could no longer work with the government. This was known as 'separation of Church and State.'

SLAVERY BECOMES ILLEGAL IN BRITAIN

ROBERT RAIKES BEGINS THE SUNDAY SCHOOL MOVEMENT

SUNDAY SCHOOLS were begun in 1764 by the English Anglican evangelical Robert Raikes. Sunday was the only day that poor children did not work, so Raikes set up a school on Sunday afternoons to teach them to read and write using the Bible as the textbook. They were also taught the catechism.

◀ **1790s** ◀ **1789-99** ◀ **1776** ◀ **1772** ◀ **1764** ◀

THE GREAT AWAKENINGS IN AMERICA

AWAKENING:

A moment of becoming suddenly aware of something.

Puritans had settled in the New England colonies during the 1600s, wanting to establish Christian towns and villages. However, as time went on and others, who were not so interested in Christianity, arrived, the zeal for serving God began to dwindle. Then in the 1730s a change began. It was very quiet at first, but it soon grew to affect all of the colonies in America.

Jonathan Edwards was a pastor of a church in Northampton, Massachusetts. He prayed and preached earnestly every week, and God began to use his sermons to convict his people of their sin and their need to confess and to serve God more faithfully. As the Holy Spirit worked in the hearts of these Christians, others began to notice the difference. They were drawn into the church wanting to know more about God. And so it spread. The more people became awakened to their need for God, the more it spread out to other towns and villages.

Other ministers also preached during that time. Theodore Frelinghuysen, a pastor and leading politician, preached to his people in New Jersey. Gilbert Tennent, a Presbyterian minister, was influenced by Frelinghuysen's preaching and formed a partnership with him. They preached in each other's churches, continuing to emphasise the importance of personal conversion. Gilbert Tennent then met George Whitfield, an English evangelist who had come to the New World to preach. Together the two men rode up and down the colonies, preaching everywhere to anyone who would listen. Whitfield also took the good news of the Gospel to slaves on the southern plantations.

Not everyone was happy about the Great Awakening. Not all ministers approved of the fiery preaching and emotional responses that some people had. These ministers tried to stop Tennent and Whitfield by refusing to allow them to use their church buildings for their meetings. So they set up outside in fields where hundreds of people would gather each time to hear the preaching of God's Word.

The Second Awakening took place half a century later. Between the two events the American Revolutionary War against Britain occurred. After America had gained its independence, society changed a great deal. Most people would still go to church, but not everyone believed in a personal God. Deism, the belief in a supreme being who didn't interfere in people's lives, became very common. America needed once more to be challenged with the Gospel.

It began on the frontier of Kentucky where James McGready, a Presbyterian minister, challenged his three little congregations with his preaching. The Holy Spirit began to work and people began to realise their need of God. So many people began to come to the churches that McGready decided to set up a huge tent and invite all of them to come for 'tent meetings' and stay overnight for several days. Many people were converted.

The awakening spread to Virginia where Presbyterians, Baptists and Methodists all cooperated to hold large meetings to preach and call people to repentance. While many were converted, there was criticism about the way some people behaved. The meetings were full of noise, people crying out, laughing loudly and falling down in their joy of hearing the Gospel.

By the 1820s the revival had spread to most of the states. Charles Finney, a great revivalist preacher, began traveling around, preaching in towns and villages. He was the first to introduce 'altar calls', challenging his hearers to show their commitment to Christ by standing or coming down to the front where Finney stood.

The 18th and 19th century revivals produced a number of notable hymn writers, all wanting to offer praise to God through the hymns they wrote.

Isaac Watts (1674-1748)

As a young man, Isaac complained that the singing in church was dull and people sang thoughtlessly. When his father heard these complaints, he challenged his son to write something better. A week later he had written his first hymn, *Behold the Glories of the Lamb*. And so began many years of writing hymns, many of them based on the Psalms.

Count Nicolaus Zinzendorf (1700-1760)

was a German nobleman, who became the leader of the Moravian church that influenced John and Charles Wesley. He wrote hymns from the time of his conversion until his death. His best known hymn is probably *Jesus, Thy Blood and Righteousness*.

Charles Wesley (1707-1788),

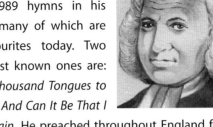

brother of John Wesley, wrote 8,989 hymns in his lifetime, many of which are still favourites today. Two of his best known ones are: *O for a Thousand Tongues to Sing* and *And Can It Be That I Should Gain*. He preached throughout England for over fifty-three years.

John Newton (1725-1807)

was a captain of a slave ship when he was converted during a storm at sea. He later left his career on the sea to study and be ordained a minister. In 1769 he started a Thursday evening prayer service at his church and wrote a new hymn each week using familiar tunes. His most famous hymn is *Amazing Grace*.

William Cowper (1731-1800)

was an English poet. He became friends with John Newton when William moved to Olney in 1771. Together they wrote hymns and eventually published the *Olney Hymns*, a collection of their hymns for churches to use.

PRAISING GOD

Fanny Crosby (1820-1915)

was an American poet and hymn writer. Being blind did not stop her from writing over 9,000 hymns during her life. She also composed some of the hymn tunes along with her husband. Two of her famous hymns are *Blessed Assurance* and *To God Be the Glory*.

Ira Sankey (1840-1908)

was known as a soloist and composer who worked with Dwight L. Moody, the evangelist. They travelled around North America and The United Kingdom, holding revival meetings. Dwight would preach and Ira would sing a solo. Ira also collaborated with hymn writers Fanny Crosby and soloist and composer Philip Bliss.

TIMELINE: MISSIONARY CHURCH 1800-1855

OVER 100 PROTESTANT FOREIGN MISSIONARIES

REVIVALS IN SCOTTISH HIGHLANDS AND SOUTHERN AMERICAN STATES

BRITISH AND FOREIGN BIBLE SOCIETY FORMED

GERMAN BIBLE SOCIETY

BIBLE SOCIETIES The first Bible Society was formed in 1804 when a group of Christians heard about Mary Jones. Mary lived in Wales and had to walk twenty miles to buy a Bible. Hearing that Bibles were difficult to find, the group formed the British and Foreign Bible Society to make sure Bibles were made available throughout the UK. They also assisted missionaries who translated the Bible into other languages to print and distribute them. Throughout the 19th century, Bible societies began to be formed in many countries.

SLAVE TRADE ABOLISHED IN THE BRITISH EMPIRE, ESPECIALLY THE ATLANTIC SLAVE TRADE

SLAVE TRADE was officially abolished by the British parliament in 1807 through the efforts of William Wilberforce and others called abolitionists. However, it was still legal to own slaves. The abolitionists continued to work to abolish slavery itself, and in 1833 the British parliament declared slavery illegal in its empire.

AMERICAN BOARD OF COMMISSIONERS OF FOREIGN MISSIONS FORMED

1800 · **1800** · **1804** · **1807** · **1810**

YWCA FORMED

In 1855 the Young Women's Christian Association was formed by Emma Robarts and Mrs. Arthur Kinnaird.

SPURGEON BECOMES PASTOR OF NEW PARK STREET CHURCH, LONDON

CHARLES SPURGEON (1834-1892) was called the Prince of Preachers. His preaching style attracted many people to his church in London, called the Metropolitan Tabernacle, which seated 5,600. He also started orphanages, alms houses (to care for the poor), and a Pastors' College to train men for the ministry.

POPE PIUS XI ISSUES 'IMMACULATE CONCEPTION' DOGMA

'IMMACULATE CONCEPTION' DOGMA Pope Pius XI and many of the bishops of the Roman Catholic Church agreed that Mary, the mother of Jesus, had been born without original sin. The pope said this dogma (or true principle) came from God. However, the Bible says nothing about Mary being sinless. She was an important person because she was chosen by God to be the mother of Jesus, but she was a sinful human being like the rest of us.

ALL FOREIGN MISSIONARIES EXPELLED FROM THAILAND

POTATO FAMINE IN IRELAND

Statue depicting famine sufferers

1855 · **1854** · **1854** · **1849** · **1845**

RUSSIAN BIBLE SOCIETY FORMED

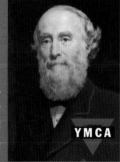

AMERICAN BIBLE SOCIETY

WESLEYAN METHODIST MISSIONARY SOCIETY FORMED

AMERICAN TRACT SOCIETY

GLASGOW CITY MISSION

City of Glasgow today

GLASGOW CITY MISSION was established in 1826 by David Nasmith to provide both physical and spiritual help to those in need. In the 1830s the mission was the first charity to offer literacy classes to help people to learn to read and write. Glasgow was the first city mission, but the idea caught on and City Missions began to start up in other cities in the UK and then throughout the world.

PLYMOUTH BRETHREN CHURCH FOUNDED

PLYMOUTH BRETHREN denomination was formed by John Nelson Darby in Plymouth, England. A group of Christians who were dissatisfied with the Anglican Church gathered to worship together without ministers or bishops. They believe in personal salvation, celebrating the Lord's supper and that the Bible is the Word of God.

1810 · **1816** · **1818** · **1825** · **1826** · **1829**

YMCA FOUNDED IN LONDON

YMCA/YWCA In 1844 twelve men led by George Williams founded the Young Men's Christian Association in London. They wanted to improve the spiritual lives of young men by offering Bible classes, prayer meetings, and lectures on how to improve their conditions.

CHRISTIAN MISSIONARIES EXPELLED FROM ETHIOPIA

DAVID LIVINGSTON ARRIVES IN BOTSWANA

ELECTRIC TELEGRAPH INVENTED

CHRISTIANS PERSECUTED IN MADAGASCAR

CHRISTIANS PERSECUTED IN MADAGASCAR In 1835 Queen Ranavalona threatened the London Missionary Society missionaries with prison if they didn't leave Madagascar immediately. After the missionaries left, she began to have Christians arrested and either executed or sent to do hard labour. In one year alone over 1,900 Christians were fined, arrested, tortured or killed. This continued until the queen died in 1861.

SLAVERY ABOLISHED IN BRITISH EMPIRE

1844 ◄ **1842** ◄ **1841** ◄ **1837** ◄ **1835** ◄ **1833**

GOING OUT INTO ALL THE WORLD

1. AFRICAN CONTINENT

George Schmidt (1709-1785) was the first Protestant missionary to go to southwestern Africa. He lived with the Khoi Khoi tribe for seven years, sharing the Gospel with them. He was then forced to leave the continent by the Dutch colonists who disagreed that African people could be saved.

Robert Moffat (1795-1883) was a Scottish missionary to South Africa for over fifty years. He translated the Bible into the tribal language of the Bechuanas. His oldest daughter married David Livingstone.

David Livingstone (1813-1873) was a Scottish medical missionary who explored much of the African continent. He opened the way for other missionaries to come in and minister to the various tribes. He also fought against the slave trade.

2. SOUTH PACIFIC

John Williams (1796-1839) was an English missionary who decided to sail to the South Pacific islands. He established churches in Tahiti, the Samoan Island, Raratonga and many other small islands. He was martyred by cannibals when he landed in the New Hebrides.

John G. Paton (1824-1907) was a Scottish missionary to the New Hebrides in the South Pacific. He worked among savage cannibals on Tanna Island. Later he moved to Aniwa Island where he

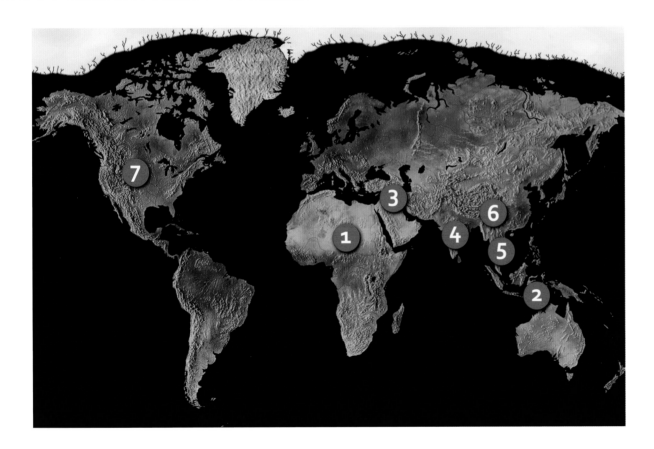

translated the New Testament and a hymnbook into their native language.

3. MIDDLE EAST

Henry Martyn (1781-1812) was an English missionary to the people of Persia and India. Inspired by William Carey, he translated the New Testament and Psalms into Persian, a language understood from the Middle East to India. He died of a fever at age 31.

Fidelia Fiske (1816-1864) was an American missionary to Persia. She established a boarding school for girls, so that they would both have an education and hear the Gospel.

She also went into the countryside to witness to the mountain tribes.

4. INDIA

William Carey (1761-1834) was an English missionary to India. He served for forty-one years as an evangelist, translator and educator. He translated the Bible into six different languages. He also founded the English Baptist Missionary Society.

Alexander Duff (1806-1878) was a Scottish missionary and educator to India. He founded schools to educate the Hindu and Muslim communities in both secular and Christian subjects.

Amy Carmichael (1867-1951) was an Irish missionary to India where she opened an orphanage and mission in Dohnavur. She remained in India for fifty-five years and wrote books about her mission work.

5. SOUTHEAST ASIA

Adoniram Judson (1788-1850) was an American missionary to Burma (called Myanmar today). During the forty years he spent in Burma he suffered persecution and imprisonment. Also, his first wife and two of his children died. He translated the Bible into Burmese.

6. CHINA

Hudson Taylor (1832-1905) was a British missionary and founder of the China Inland Mission. He took the radical step of dressing like the Chinese people he lived with.

Other missionaries at that time thought this was foolish. He was also one of the first to go into the interior of China to reach mountain tribes.

Robert Morrison (1782-1834) was an English missionary to China. He 1813 he completed the translation of the New Testament into the common Chinese language.

Charlotte (Lottie) Moon (1840-1912) was an American missionary to northern China, around Tengchow and Pingtu. She taught Chinese children and evangelised Chinese women for forty years.

7. NORTH AMERICA

David Brainerd (1718-1747) was an American missionary to the Native American tribes in the northeast of what is the USA today. He started a school for Native American  children in New York colony and then ministered to the Delaware tribe in the Pennsylvania colony. He died of tuberculosis at age twenty-nine.

Peter Jones (1802-1856) was half Welsh and half Native Canadian. He was converted at twenty-one and ordained as a minister in the Methodist church. He preached in Upper Canada to the native peoples in their own language and assisted with translating the Bible into the Mississauga language.

TIMELINE: **MISSIONARY CHURCH 1856-1900**

CHARLES DARWIN PUBLISHES *THE ORIGIN OF THE SPECIES*

REVIVAL IN SOUTH AFRICA

REVIVAL IN SOUTH AFRICA (1860-62) After years of prayer for revival, Andrew Murray conducted a church conference in Worcester in South Africa. During the conference people began to pray in earnest and even when Mr. Murray tried to stop the meeting, the praying continued. Over the next two years the revival spread through the cities and into the villages and farms. It was described as a firestorm that transformed society.

AMERICAN CIVIL WAR

SEVENTH DAY ADVENTIST CHURCH FORMED

CHINA INLAND MISSION FOUNDED BY HUDSON TAYLOR

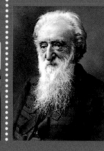

SALVATION ARMY FOUNDED BY WILLIAM BOOTH

FIRST VATICAN COUNCIL

FIRST VATICAN COUNCIL Pope Pius IX called the council of bishops together in 1869 to deal with problems in the Roman Catholic Church. At the end of the council, they announced that whenever the Pope spoke about church matters, he was speaking for God and was therefore 'infallible' (never wrong). There is no basis for papal infallibility in the Bible.

1859	1860-62	1861-65	1864	1865	1865	1869

CHRISTIAN COMMERCIAL TRAVELLERS ASSOCIATION OF AMERICA (GIDEON INTERNATIONAL) FORMED

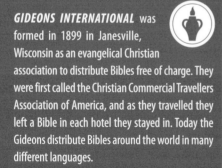

GIDEONS INTERNATIONAL was formed in 1899 in Janesville, Wisconsin as an evangelical Christian association to distribute Bibles free of charge. They were first called the Christian Commercial Travellers Association of America, and as they travelled they left a Bible in each hotel they stayed in. Today the Gideons distribute Bibles around the world in many different languages.

CHRISTIANS MASSACRED BY TURKS

CHRISTIANS MASSACRED BY TURKS From 1894-1897 Christians in the Ottoman Empire were systematically killed by Sultan Abdul Hamid II, who thought Christians were a threat to his empire. He also included many Armenian people in his massacres.

SUDAN INTERIOR MISSION BEGINS

SUDAN INTERIOR MISSION was founded in 1893 by Canadians Walter Gowans and Roland Bingham and American Thomas Kent. The three men went to the sub-Sahara in west Africa, an area that had never been visited by missionaries. Gowans and Kent died of malaria the next year, but Bingham returned to Canada. Prevented by ill health from returning, he sent out a missionary team, who established a base for the mission in the interior.

STUDENT VOLUNTEER MOVEMENT FOR FOREIGN MISSIONS FORMED IN USA

VOLUNTEER STUDENT MOVEMENT BEGINS

250 CHRISTIANS EXECUTED IN UGANDA

CHRISTIANS EXECUTED IN UGANDA King Mwanga II came to the Ugandan throne in 1884. He viewed Christian missionaries (Protestant and Roman Catholic) as a threat, so he had them expelled from his country. Over the next several years, he executed 250 Anglican and Roman Catholic Ugandans who refused to recant their faith.

1899	1894-1897	1893	1888	1886	1885

JEHOVAH'S WITNESSES FOUNDED

JEHOVAH'S WITNESSES Around 1870 Charles Russell became interested in studying the Bible to look for Christ's return. He formed a Bible study in Pittsburgh, PA and by 1879 was calling himself a pastor and publishing a magazine called *The Watchtower*. Eventually they became known as Jehovah's Witnesses. They do not believe in eternal life, the Trinity or that Jesus is the Son of God. They are heretics.

RUSSIAN ORTHODOX CHURCH ESTABLISHES FIRST DIOCESE IN AMERICA

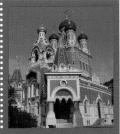

GREAT FIRE OF CHICAGO DESTROYS 50 CHURCHES AND MISSIONS

REVIVALS IN JAPAN

MOODY AND SANKEY BEGIN THEIR CRUSADES

DWIGHT L. MOODY (1837-1899) was converted at the YMCA at age eighteen. He established a mission church in Chicago, but thirteen years later it was destroyed in the Great Chicago Fire. From then on Moody began to preach in various cities in North America and Europe. Ira Sankey, a soloist and hymn writer, joined him and together they held 'crusades' (enormous meetings) preaching to thousands at a time. He also established schools, including the Moody Bible Institute.

CHRISTIANITY LEGALISED IN JAPAN

In 1867 Emperor Meiji inherited the Japanese throne from his father. He was a reformer and over time changed the feudal society ruled by various shoguns (military leaders) to a central government that allowed trade with western countries. As a result, Christian missionaries, who had been banned since the 1600s, were allowed to come into Japan.

1870 ··· **1871** ··· **1871** ··· **1872** ··· **1873**

TREATY BETWEEN USA AND KOREA ALLOWS RELIGIOUS FREEDOM

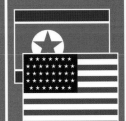

CHRISTIAN SCIENCE MOVEMENT FOUNDED

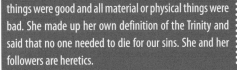

THE CHRISTIAN SCIENCE MOVEMENT was founded in Boston in 1879 by Mary Baker Eddy. She taught her followers that only spiritual things were good and all material or physical things were bad. She made up her own definition of the Trinity and said that no one needed to die for our sins. She and her followers are heretics.

SCRIPTURE UNION FORMED

INTERVARSITY CHRISTIAN FELLOWSHIP BEGINS IN UK

KESWICK CONVENTION BEGINS IN ENGLAND

1885 ◀ **1882** ◀ **1879** ◀ **1879** ◀ **1877** ◀ **1875** ◀ **1873**

SCIENCE AND THE BIBLE

Since Medieval times scientific discoveries were being made regularly. From the 1500s onward, astronomers and mathematicians like Nicolaus Copernicus, Galileo Galilei and Isaac Newton were making scientific discoveries about the earth and the universe. Ideas began to change. The world around didn't seem so mysterious when science could explain why something happened. People began to think that everything about the universe could be explained and understood, including God.

This became known as the scientific revolution.

Faced with all of these new discoveries, some people began to think that Christianity was outdated, or at least the Bible should be looked at in a new way. The meaning or understanding of 'truth' was changing. Here's how the argument would go:

Before the scientific revolution everyone thought the earth was the centre of the universe. That was considered a 'true' saying. When scientists discovered that the earth was only one very small part of the universe, then that 'true' saying was no longer true and had to be changed. So (and here is where it starting to go terribly wrong) people began to look at the Bible and say, 'It's been around a long time. Maybe it isn't as true as we thought.'

At that point, some Christians in the 19th century began to worry that science would show that God's Word, the Bible, was wrong after all. So they began to think of ways to defend Christianity. Unfortunately, their attempts made it even worse.

Friedrich Schleiermacher (1768-1834) thought the best way to defend Christianity was to change a few things. Instead of saying the Bible was God's only way of speaking to people, he said that a person's feelings and reasoning (or thinking) were also important. The Bible was just a guideline. That is very dangerous, because as sinful human beings we often get things wrong and need God's Word to tell us what is right and wrong. Friedrich also said that Jesus was an important moral teacher, but probably not really divine. And here is where he became a heretic, because Jesus is divine, the Son of God.

Later in the century, Charles Darwin published his *The Origin of the Species*. He, along with others, developed the theory that all life had evolved from primitive forms of life into human beings. In other words, rather than each species (or type) of life on earth being individually created by God, they just developed on their own. If what Charles had written was true, then there was no need for a creator.

Sadly many people thought Schleiermacher and Darwin knew the 'truth' and used that as an excuse to reject Christianity. And even worse, some Christians began to write about and teach these ideas as part of Christianity. They were causing the most harm by trying to confuse the church.

William Booth, a Methodist minister, and his wife Catherine, became concerned about the poor people in East London. William resigned from his church in 1865 to preach to them and offer practical help. He was planning to send converts to the churches in the area. However, he soon realised that would not work. Churches in 19th century Britain charged a pew tax, which poor people could not afford. Nor could the poor afford good clothing, which most church members thought was very important. So William started a church just for the new Christians called the East London Christian Mission.

In 1878 William's son, Bramwell, suggested changing the name of the church. William had written in a report that 'The Christian Mission was a volunteer army.' When Bramwell saw it, he crossed out the word volunteer because he said that he wasn't just a volunteer; he was compelled by his love for Christ to work for Him. So instead of volunteer, he wrote 'salvation.' Soon the name became the Salvation Army. Their leaders became

MARCHING FOR GOD

known as generals and other officer titles. In that same year, brass instruments were used in their worship services and in the streets as they marched and sang hymns.

What made the Salvation Army different from some churches was its efforts to help people in practical ways. They offered food to the hungry; they helped the homeless find places to live; they visited those in prisons and helped their families. And all the while they shared the Gospel, offering hope to those who felt hopeless.

By the 1880s the Salvation Army had spread to America, Canada, Australia, Asia, Africa and India. Their leaders were called Generals, rather than ministers. Many people laughed at the Salvation Army, saying it was just a ragged bunch of people. When the Salvation Army went into dangerous places in cities, they often faced violence from the very people they wanted to help. But they went anyway, knowing that God wanted these people to hear the Gospel too.

MODERN
CHURCH

REVIVAL IN KOREA

IT ALL STARTED WITH A PRAYER MEETING.

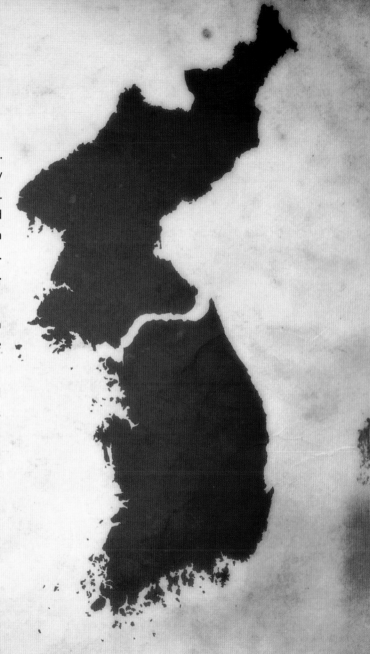

estern missionaries had been working in Korea for many years. By 1906 they had some converts and had built a few churches in the main cities and mission stations in the rural areas. In that year some Presbyterian and Methodist missionaries, who lived and worked in Ping Yang, decided to start praying together regularly at noon. After a month, when nothing out of the ordinary began to happen, one of them suggested they stop because it interrupted the missionaries' work. But rather than stop, the group decided to move the prayer meeting to 4 p.m. and pray until suppertime. They prayed every day for six months, asking God to bring revival to the Korean churches and bring about many conversions in the cities and countryside.

In January 1907 something happened during a special week of prayer at Central Presbyterian Church in Ping Yang. Right in the middle of the service, Elder Keel stood up. Everyone was startled at the interruption and even more startled when he began to speak. He told the church that he was like Achan from the Old Testament, who had stolen money and clothing when the Israelites had conquered Jericho. Elder Keel said that God would not bless the church until he confessed his sin: he had stolen money

from a widow and he now promised to give it back. After he sat down there was silence, and then slowly others in the congregation stood up one at a time. They each confessed how they too had sinned against God. The church service, which had begun at 7 p.m., didn't end until 2 a.m. the next morning. Over the next few months people began to change. They returned what had been stolen.

They forgave those who had hurt them. Even a known robber turned himself into police after he was converted.

By the middle of the year over 30,000 people had been converted to Christianity and the churches in Ping Yang were overflowing. The revival spread out to the rest of the country. Missionaries were overjoyed. Just like at Pentecost, when the Holy Spirit came to the disciples meeting in the upper room, so the Holy Spirit was convicting and calling thousands of people to repentance and faith. Churches were so full they had to have several services each day. Whole villages in the rural areas were converted.

When the news of the Korean revival reached Manchuria, two missionaries travelled down to Ping Yang to find out about it. When they asked what special things the missionaries had done to bring about the revival, the answer was 'prayer.' When they asked about how the Gospel was spread, the answer was, 'every Christian evangelises his neighbour.'

TIMELINE: MODERN CHURCH 1900-1938

BOXER REBELLION IN CHINA

BOXER REBELLION (1900) was a violent Chinese revolt against foreigners in general and missionaries in particular. The group who started the rebellion were called 'the Militia United in Righteousness', but were known in English as 'Boxers.' They were angry at foreigners trying to take over their country, and tried to drive all non-Chinese people out. Over 180 missionaries were killed, and churches were burned. The rebellion was put down by international troops after three months.

AMERICAN STANDARD VERSION BIBLE PUBLISHED

REVIVAL IN KOREA

MANCHURIAN REVIVAL

MANCHURIAN REVIVAL (1908) Jonathan Goforth, a Canadian Presbyterian missionary who survived the Boxer Rebellion, travelled to Manchuria to speak at a series of church meetings. After four days, the congregation began to respond, confessing their sins to God and each other. The effects of the revival spread out from the churches to the towns and villages. Some even said, 'Don't go near those Christians! Their Spirit has come down and is irresistible.'

FIRST WORLD MISSIONARY CONFERENCE

FIRST WORLD MISSIONARY CONFERENCE (1910) Delegates from 176 missionary societies around the world met in June 1910 in Edinburgh. For ten days they met for daily prayer and discussions on ways to evangelise the non-Christian world. The

1900 • **1901** • **1907** • **1908** • **1910**

AMERICAN CHAPTER OF INTERVARSITY FOUNDED

WYCLIFFE BIBLE TRANSLATORS FOUNDED

Wycliffe Bible Translators

WYCLIFFE BIBLE TRANSLATORS (1934) was founded by Cameron Townsend. In 1917 he went to Guatemala to sell Spanish Bibles, but soon discovered none of the tribespeople spoke Spanish, and most did not have a written language. He founded Wycliffe Bible Translators to send missionaries to tribes around the world that had no written language, to write out their languages and translate the Bible for them.

HCJB RADIO STATION BEGINS IN QUITO, ECUADOR

HCJB RADIO STATION BEGAN IN QUITO, ECUADOR (1931) HCJB was the first Christian short-wave radio station, which meant it was able to be heard over very long distances. American evangelists Clarence Jones and Reuben Larsen began broadcasting on Christmas Day in 1931, offering programming in English as well as foreign languages. The broadcasts could be heard around the world with a short-wave radio receiver.

WESTMINSTER THEOLOGICAL SEMINARY IN PHILADELPHIA FOUNDED

WESTMINSTER THEOLOGICAL SEMINARY IN PHILADELPHIA FOUNDED (1929) Princeton Seminary, originally a Presbyterian college, began to introduce liberal theology in the first part of the 20th century. In 1929 J. Gresham Machen, and other conservative faculty members, left Princeton and founded Westminster Theological Seminary in order to continue teaching the Reformed faith.

1938 • **1934** • **1931** • **1929**

delegates decided not to discuss doctrinal matters that they disagreed with, but rather focus on practical ways of doing mission work. This was the beginning of the Ecumenical Movement.

WORLD WAR I

RUSSIAN REVOLUTION TURNS RUSSIA INTO A COMMUNIST STATE

Demonstration of workers at Putilovskogo factory on the first day of the Revolution of 1917

FIRST CHURCH SERVICE BROADCAST ON RADIO

FIRST CHURCH SERVICE BROADCAST ON RADIO (1921) In January 1921, two months after radio broadcasting began in the USA, Station KDKA in Pittsburgh, Pennsylvania, aired Calvary Episcopal Church's morning worship service. This was the first religious service ever broadcasted.

NCRV, FIRST INTERNATIONAL CHRISTIAN RADIO STATION BEGINS IN THE NETHERLANDS

SCOPES TRIAL IN AMERICA

SCOPES MONKEY TRIAL IN AMERICA (1925) A high school teacher, John Scopes, was arrested for illegally teaching the theory of evolution. His trial attracted national attention. Scopes was convicted and fined $100. However, the trial lawyer, Clarence Darrow, successfully ridiculed the Bible and Christians in the courtroom, which was published in all the newspapers. This trial was the first step toward changing the school curriculum. Eventually schools no longer taught Creation, saying the theory of evolution was true and the Bible was not.

1910 **1914-18** **1917** **1921** **1924**

STALIN BECOMES DICTATOR IN SOVIET UNION

STALIN BECAME DICTATOR IN SOVIET UNION (1929) Joseph Stalin was noted for his brutality to anyone who did not agree with him. His plans to change the Soviet Union from an agricultural country to an industrialised one worked, but it also resulted in great suffering for the Soviet people. By the time of his death in 1953, over 20 million people, including many Christians, had died in labour camps, from execution or from starvation.

POPE PIUS XI ISSUES MORTALIUM ANIMOS [MINDS OF MEN OR MORTAL SOULS]

POPE PIUS XI ISSUED MORTALIUM ANIMOS [MINDS OF MEN OR MORTAL SOULS] (1928) The Roman Catholic church was invited to participate in some of the ecumenical meetings of some Protestant churches. Pope Pius XI responded with a document, Mortalium Animos which is Latin for Minds of Men or Mortal Souls, refusing to join the meetings. He said that ignoring doctrinal beliefs in order to have unity was dangerous and would lead to error. Although he was referring to what the Roman Catholic Church believes, he was right about the dangers of the Ecumenical Movement.

CANADIAN CHAPTER OF INTERVARSITY FOUNDED

1929 **1928** **1928** **1925**

ECUMENICALISM AND THE SOCIAL GOSPEL

ECUMENICALISM:

is another word for unity, literally meaning 'from the whole world'.

In the 20th century the world was becoming more connected with the introduction of radio and later television, and travel became easier with improved ships and planes. People began to talk about a global society, where everyone was connected to everyone else. The churches too began to think in global terms.

It started at the 1910 Edinburgh World Missionary Conference. Missionaries around the world kept 'bumping into each other' on the mission field. Sometimes Baptists, Anglicans or Presbyterians set up missions in the same place, but then failed to work well together. The Edinburgh conference was an attempt to solve this problem. However, since not all denominations agreed on doctrinal issues,

they decided not to talk about doctrine. Instead, they wanted everyone to focus on the life and work of the church, its social ministries of helping the poor, the orphan and the widow.

These ideas continued to be important to some churches, so in 1948 they formed the World Council of Churches. They used a verse from Jesus' prayer in John 17:21 as their motto: *that they may all be one, just as you, Father, are in me, and I in you, that they also may be in us*.

They saw that the church was split into so many denominations and they wanted to bring everyone back into one unified church. However, to do so meant dropping any doctrine that they could not all agree on. When you start doing that, then you are not left with very much that the Bible teaches. The World Council of Churches said what mattered was doing the work of the church and not fighting over doctrine. Unity became more important than God's Word.

SOCIAL GOSPEL

At the same time there was a movement afoot in North America called the Social Gospel. Christian people were becoming more and more concerned about social problems such as poverty, crime, alcoholism, child labour and inequalities in society. They began to use the verse in Matthew 6:10: *Thy kingdom come, thy will be done on earth as it is in heaven* as their reason for focusing on these issues. They thought that Jesus would not return until these problems were fixed, but in their efforts to help those in need, they forgot the real purpose of the church: to glorify God and preach the Gospel as found in the Bible.

Just as Christians were imprisoned or killed for their faith during the Early Church times, it is the same in the Modern Church. Islamic countries make it illegal to be a Christian or evangelise. Dictators won't tolerate Christians obeying God before them. Listed below are some of the places around the world that Christians have been suffering in the last hundred years. We should remember to pray for our brothers and sisters who live under such conditions.

MODERN MARTYRS

SOVIET UNION (NOW RUSSIA):

In 1917 the Communists came to power in Russia after the October Revolution. Leon Trotsky, one of the leaders, issued orders to have twenty-eight bishops and 1200 priests killed. Communism rejected all religions and tried to replace them with atheism. Later, when Joseph Stalin became the leader in 1929, he ordered his secret police to search out Christians and arrest them. The worst purges were during 1937-38 when 100,000 clergy were shot and killed.

CHINA:

During China's Cultural Revolution (1966-76) many Christians were put in prison or executed. Government soldiers destroyed all the Bibles they could find and looted the homes of Christians. Again in 1983 hundreds of church leaders were arrested and house-church meetings made illegal.

GERMANY:

From 1933-45 Germany was ruled by Adolph Hitler. While he is mainly known for his hatred of Jews and his systematic plan to kill them all, he was no more sympathetic to Christians who spoke out against his government. Early in WWII, Hitler had many Roman Catholic priests and Protestant pastors arrested and sent to Dachau concentration camp, where most died of starvation or disease.

SUDAN:

In 1983 Roman Catholic and Anglican clergy signed a declaration that said they would not stop serving God even though they were threatened with death by the Muslim government. The government soldiers then began to murder pastors and church leaders, bomb churches during Sunday services, and destroy Christian mission bases, hospitals and schools. This persecution of Christians is still going on today.

UGANDA:

During Idi Amin's reign (1971-1979) over 40,000 Christians were either killed or disappeared.

TIMELINE: MODERN CHURCH 1939-1965

WORLD WAR II

YOUTH FOR CHRIST FOUNDED

DIETRICH BONHOEFFER EXECUTED BY NAZIS

DIETRICH BONHOEFFER EXECUTED BY NAZIS (1945) Dietrich Bonhoeffer was a German pastor and professor. He was arrested during World War 2 by German soldiers for opposing Hitler and Nazism. After spending almost two years in prison and concentration camps, he was tried and executed for treason.

FIRST URBANA STUDENT MISSION CONFERENCE

FIRST URBANA STUDENT MISSION CONFERENCE (1946) was held in Toronto. Sponsored by InterVarsity, the conference hosted students from around North America. The conference featured speakers that introduced students to foreign missions and the part they could play. The next conference, in 1948, moved to the University of Illinois in Urbana. The conference used the name 'Urbana' from then onward.

DEAD SEA SCROLLS DISCOVERED

DEAD SEA SCROLLS DISCOVERED (1947) These ancient manuscripts were first discovered by a Bedouin shepherd in caves near Jerusalem. They had been stored in large jars over 2,000 years old, the oldest manuscripts of Old Testament texts that we have.

1939-1945 · 1944 · 1945 · 1946 · 1946/47

SECOND VATICAN COUNCIL

SECOND VATICAN COUNCIL (1962-65) was called by Pope John XXIII to discuss the church's role in the 20th century. Popularly called Vatican 2, the council did not change any significant Roman Catholic doctrine, but a number of changes were made to the church's worship and practice. Permission was given to say the mass in the language of the people instead of Latin. More Scripture readings were added to the mass and the people were encouraged to study their Bibles.

CBN, FIRST CHRISTIAN TELEVISION STATION

CBN, FIRST CHRISTIAN TELEVISION STATION (1961) was launched by Pat Robertson in Portsmouth, Virginia. At first it only aired programming in the evening, until more supporters could be found. In 1963 he hosted a telethon to raise enough money to remain on the air because he refused to take commercial advertising. Enough money was raised and its Gospel programming is seen around the world.

JIM ELLIOT MARTYRED

VIETNAM WAR

BANNER OF TRUTH MAGAZINE BEGINS

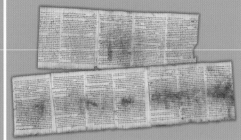

BANNER OF TRUTH MAGAZINE BEGAN (1955) Sidney Norton and Iain Murray decided to edit a magazine to help strengthen the church in the United Kingdom. They decided to publish Puritan authors as well as the works of George Whitfield and Charles Spurgeon. Dr Martyn Lloyd-Jones and Westminster Chapel also assisted by covering half the production costs.

1962-65 · 1961 · 1956 · 1955-75 · 1955

WORLD COUNCIL OF CHURCHES ESTABLISHED

WORLD COUNCIL OF CHURCHES (1948) was established when 147 churches came together at their first assembly in Amsterdam. They wanted to promote their common witness in mission work and evangelism. While the idea was a good one, the only way it could work was for churches to ignore doctrines they disagreed on and focus only on social issues.

BILLY GRAHAM'S FIRST CRUSADE

BILLY GRAHAM'S FIRST CRUSADE (1949) Rev. Billy Graham set up a 'canvas cathedral' (two circus tents put together) in Los Angeles, California for a series of evangelistic meetings. The crusade, as it came to be called, lasted eight weeks and more than 350,000 people attended. This began his career of evangelistic crusades throughout the world, which he continued until he retired in 2000.

CHINESE COMMUNIST REVOLUTION

MOTHER TERESA FORMS MISSIONARIES OF CHARITY ORDER

WORLD VISION FORMED

World Vision®

WORLD VISION (1950) Bob Pierce, an American Baptist minister and relief worker, founded World Vision primarily to care for children orphaned by the Korean War. Within ten years it had expanded to caring for over 65,000 children in twenty countries.

1948	1949	1949	1950	1950

FRANCIS SCHAEFFER FOUNDS L'ABRI

L'ABRI

FRANCIS SCHAEFFER FOUNDS L'ABRI (1955) Francis and Edith Schaeffer began L'Abri Fellowship by opening their home in Switzerland to travellers who wanted to ask questions about Christianity. L'Abri means 'shelter' in French. When more and more people began to arrive, L'Abri expanded to include more buildings to allow people to remain for several months at a time.

MERE CHRISTIANITY BY C S LEWIS PUBLISHED

WORLD WIDE PICTURES FOUNDED BY BILLY GRAHAM

RUINS OF QUMRAN UNCOVERED

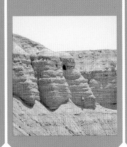

CAMPUS CRUSADE FOR CHRIST FOUNDED

cru

CAMPUS CRUSADE FOR CHRIST (1951) was founded by Bill and Vonette Bright on the UCLA campus. Bill was a student at Fuller Theological Seminary and felt called by God to reach the world, starting with college students. This evangelistic outreach spread to other college and high school campuses. In 1958 the organisation became international when Campus Crusade for Christ began operating in Korea.

1955	1952	1952	1951	1951

IMPORTANT PEOPLE IN THE MODERN CHURCH

Evangeline Booth (1865-1950) was the daughter of William and Catherine Booth, the founders of the Salvation Army. She was director of the Army operations in Canada for eight years and then in the USA for twenty years. She was especially concerned for the homeless, alcoholics, unwed mothers and neglected children. She was also commended for her work with American troops during WW1.

J. Gresham Machen (1881-1937) was an American Presbyterian theologian. He was a New Testament scholar and taught at Princeton Seminary from 1906-29. When other professors at Princeton began to teach modernist theology, he and other conservative faculty members left to form Westminster Theological Seminary in 1929. He was also instrumental in forming the Orthodox Presbyterian Church in 1936.

John Murray (1898-1975) was a Scottish theologian who taught systematic theology for one year at Princeton Seminary before following J. Gresham Machen to form Westminster Theological Seminary. He taught there from 1930-1966 and wrote a number of books on theology that are still used today in seminaries.

C.S. Lewis (1898-1963) was an Irish academic, novelist, poet and lay theologian who taught at Oxford and Cambridge Universities. He is best known for *The Chronicles of Narnia*, a series of children's fantasy books with Christian themes. His book *Mere Christianity* was based on a series of radio talks he gave, and has been instrumental in many conversions.

Martyn Lloyd-Jones (1899-1981) was a Welsh minister and medical doctor. He served as minister of Westminster Chapel in London for almost thirty years. He was a gifted preacher and taught the Reformed faith to thousands every year. His sermons are still read today.

Billy Graham (1918-) is an American evangelist, best known for his crusades that he has held around the world. He began preaching on the radio and then in 1949 held his first crusade in Los Angeles. Since then he has preached the Gospel faithfully and written many books and articles. He retired in 2000.

Gladys Aylward (1902-1970) was a British missionary to China. Along with Jeannie Lawson, she established an inn for travellers, serving both food and the gospel.

During the war between China and Japan, Gladys also began to take in orphans and wounded soldiers, caring for them as best she could. When the Japanese invaded the area where she worked, she took the 100 children in her care across the mountains to safety. She was forced to leave China by the Communist government in 1947. She finished her days in Taiwan, caring for children in an orphanage.

John Stott (1921-2011) was an English Anglican vicar who was rector of All Souls Church in London for twenty-five years. He was one of the authors of the Lausanne Covenant in 1974. He was an influential evangelical leader who wrote over fifty books that have been translated into seventy-two languages. He founded the Langham Partnership to fund young evangelical preachers and provide theological literature for developing countries.

J.I. Packer (1926-) is a British-born Canadian theologian. He taught systematic theology at Regent College in Vancouver and preached widely in the UK and North America. He has written over 165 books and numerous articles that have been helpful to many Christians, as well as instrumental in many conversions.

Francis Schaeffer (1912-1984) was an American Presbyterian minister and philosopher. He is best known for establishing L'Abri in Switzerland for those searching for answers about life. He and his wife Edith hosted many people over the years and presented them with the Gospel. Both Francis and Edith wrote numerous books about Christian living and theology.

Elisabeth Elliot (1926-2015) was an American missionary and writer. Her first husband, Jim Elliot, was murdered by Auca tribesmen in Ecuador. Elisabeth, later, went to live with the Auca people and preach the Gospel. When she returned to the United States, she became a speaker and writer, particularly to women. She emphasised contentment in Christ and recognising that God is in control of all things.

BURMA EXPELS MISSIONARIES

ALBANIA BECOMES THE FIRST OFFICIAL ATHEIST STATE

JESUS MOVEMENT BEGINS

North American Street, USA, 1960s

JESUS MOVEMENT BEGAN (1968) in the United States and spread throughout North America, Europe and Central America. It was made up of former drug addicts, hippies, people involved in the occult, musicians and many others who had become Christians. They didn't feel comfortable in churches and preferred to be involved in outreach ministries in inner cities and places where many churches didn't evangelise.

THE HIDING PLACE BY CORRIE TEN BOOM PUBLISHED

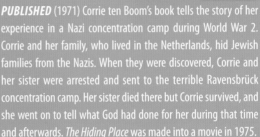

THE HIDING PLACE BY CORRIE TEN BOOM PUBLISHED (1971) Corrie ten Boom's book tells the story of her experience in a Nazi concentration camp during World War 2. Corrie and her family, who lived in the Netherlands, hid Jewish families from the Nazis. When they were discovered, Corrie and her sister were arrested and sent to the terrible Ravensbrück concentration camp. Her sister died there but Corrie survived, and she went on to tell what God had done for her during that time and afterwards. *The Hiding Place* was made into a movie in 1975.

FIRST INTERNATIONAL CONGRESS ON WORLD EVANGELISM IN LAUSANNE

FIRST INTERNATIONAL CONGRESS ON WORLD EVANGELISM (1974) met in Lausanne, Switzerland. A committee, headed by Billy Graham, invited over 2,300 evangelical leaders from 150

1966   **1966**   **1968**   **1971**   **1974**

ENGLISH STANDARD VERSION BIBLE PUBLISHED

ESV
STUDY BIBLE

GLOBAL NETWORK OF MISSION STRUCTURES

GLOBAL NETWORK OF MISSION STRUCTURES (2005) began as an agency to help local denominations around the world to organise mission work. It assists with recruiting, training and mentoring missionaries. And they also help field leaders and directors with the challenges of missionary work.

NEW TRIBES MISSIONARIES MARTIN AND GRACIA BURNHAM KIDNAPPED IN PHILIPPIANS BY MUSLIM TERRORIST GROUP

THIRD INTERNATIONAL CONFERENCE FOR ITINERANT EVANGELISTS

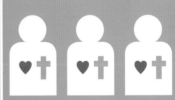

THIRD INTERNATIONAL CONFERENCE FOR ITINERANT EVANGELISTS (2000) met in Amsterdam for a nine-day conference. Over 10,000 evangelists from many countries attended. The emphasis of the conference was on correct theology preached by godly evangelists, and not to compromise the truth of God's Word.

BACK TO JERUSALEM SENDS OUT 36 CHINESE MISSIONARIES

BACK TO JERUSALEM MOVEMENT (2000) began as an idea in the 1920s in mainland China. Chinese believers wanted to send out missionaries to the Buddhist, Hindu and Muslim people who lived between

2008   **2005**   **2001**   **2000**   **2000**

countries to attend. The congress drew up the Lausanne Covenant, which stated the .biblical doctrines they all shared and a desire to spread the Gospel around the world. The congress has continued to meet in Manila in 1989 and Cape Town in 2010.

FOREIGN MISSIONARIES EXPELLED FROM CAMBODIA AND VIETNAM

NEW INTERNATIONAL VERSION BIBLE PUBLISHED

NIV BIBLE PUBLISHED (1978)
Plans for translation work for the NIV Bible began in 1965. Evangelical scholars used the best Greek, Hebrew and Aramaic manuscripts for their translation work. In 1973 they published the New Testament, and in 1978 the full Bible translation was completed.

MOTHER TERESA AWARDED NOBEL PEACE PRIZE

WORLD EVANGELISM CRUSADE IN SEOUL, KOREA [ATTENDANCE: 16.2 MILLION]

WORLD EVANGELISM CRUSADE IN SEOUL, KOREA (1980) was held at Yoido Plaza, which had been used as an airport during World War II. It was twenty-one miles wide and one mile long. Over the week-long series of meetings 16.5 million people attended. 700,000 people were converted.

1974   **1975**   **1978**   **1979**   **1980**

China and Jerusalem. However, persecution by the Chinese government made it difficult to carry out. In 2000 the movement was able to send out thirty-six missionaries westward to begin the mission.

BILLY GRAHAM'S AUTOBIOGRAPHY *JUST AS I AM* PUBLISHED

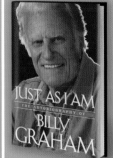

COLLAPSE OF COMMUNISM IN RUSSIA AND EASTERN EUROPE [POST-SOVIET RUSSIAN GOVERNMENT RESTORES RELIGIOUS FREEDOM]

Berlin wall, before it fell on 9th November 1989

NEW REVISED STANDARD VERSION BIBLE PUBLISHED

NEW KING JAMES VERSION BIBLE PUBLISHED

NEW KING JAMES BIBLE PUBLISHED (1982) A team of 130 scholars, editors, church leaders and Christian laity began work on the New King James Version in 1975. The New Testament was completed in 1979, the Book of Psalms in 1980, and the full Bible in 1982.

2000   **1997**   **1990**   **1989**   **1982**

CONCLUSION

Christ's church is almost 2,000 years old. She has experienced times of great blessing and times of great difficulty, either from persecution without or from heresy within. Many kingdoms have come and gone and many leaders have lived and died throughout human history. Yet the church still exists today. Nothing that is started by people is permanent. But Christ's church is different. The kingdom that Jesus established with his death and resurrection is a permanent one, because God himself is the founder. His kingdom will not pass away as human ones have, but will continue until Jesus returns.

We can learn many lessons from our past, from zealous Christians who have tried to live as God commands us, and from those who have opposed God's kingdom. We can see what is right and what is wrong. We should also be encouraged that even when the church is under attack from people who think they know better, God is still in control. Jesus gave this promise to the Apostle Peter and to every Christian down through history:

Simon Peter replied, 'You are the Christ, the Son of the living God.' And Jesus answered him, 'Blessed are you, Simon Bar-Jonah! For flesh and blood has not revealed this to you, but my Father who is in heaven. And I tell you, you are Peter, and on this rock I will build my church, and the gates of hell shall not prevail against it.'

Matthew 16:17-18

BIBLIOGRAPHY

BOOKS

Aland, Kurt. *Saints and Sinners: men and ideas in the early church*. Philadelphia, Fortress Press, 1970

Bellitto, Christopher M. *Church History 101: a concise overview*. Liguori, Missouri, Liguori, 2008

Bhote, Tehmina. *Charlemagne: the life and times of an early medieval emperor*. NY, The Rosen Publishing Group, 2005.

Chadwick, Henry. *The Early Church*. (The Pelican History of the Church:1) London, Penguin Books, 1967

Chadwick, Owen. *The Reformation* (The Pelican History of the Church: 3). Harmondsworth, UK, Penguin Books Ltd., 1969.

Carins, Earle E. *Christianity Through the Centuries: a history of the Christian church edited*. 3rd edition, rev. and expanded. Grand Rapids, MI, Zondervan, 1996.

Cragg, Gerald R. *The Church and the Age of Reason 1648-1789* (The Pelican History of the Church: 4). Harmondsworth, UK, Penguin Books Ltd., 1970.

Hannah, John D. *Charts of Modern and Postmodern Church History*. Grand Rapids, Zondervan Publishing House, 2004.

Hannah, John D. *Charts of Reformation and Enlightenment Church History*. Grand Rapids, Zondervan Publishing House, 2004.

Neill, Stephen. *The History of Christian Missions* (The Pelican History of the Church: 6). Harmondsworth, UK, Penguin Books Ltd., 1964.

The Oxford Illustrated History of Christianity, edited by John McManners. New York, Oxford University Press, 1990.

Petersen, Susan Lynn. *Timeline Charts of the Western Church*. Grand Rapids, Zondervan Publishing House, 1999.

Scherman, Katharine. *The Birth of France: warriors, bishops and long-haired kings*. NY, Random House, 1987.

Southern, R.W. *Western Society and the Church in the Middle Ages*. (The Pelican History of the Church: 2) London, Penguin Books, 1970.

Stark, Rodney. *God's Battalions: the case for the crusades*. NY, Harper Collins Publishers, 2009.

Wilken, Robert Louis. *The First Thousand Years: a global history of Christianity*. New Haven, Yale University Press, 2012.

USEFUL WEBSITES

'Christian History.' Christianity Today. Accessed July 2, 2016 http://www.christianitytoday.com/history.

'Church History Timeline.' Christianity.com. Accessed September 1, 2016. http://www.christianity.com/church/church-history/timeline/.

History. Accessed September 28, 2016 http://www.history.com

IMAGE INDEX

Page	Timeline Year	Timeline entry / Section	Image license attribution
40	1545-1563	Council of Trent	By Laurom (Own work) [CC BY-SA 3.0], via Wikimedia Commons
41	1536	William Tyndale sentenced to death	By John Foxe [Public domain], via Wikimedia Commons
41	1536	William Tyndale sentenced to death	By Tohma (Own work) [CC BY-SA 4.0-3.0-2.5-2.0-1.0], via Wikimedia Commons
41	1536	Calvin becomes pastor in Geneva for the first time	Formerly attributed to Hans Holbein [Public domain], via Wikimedia Commons
41	1536	Denmark-Norway become Lutheran	By Sodacan. Vector image created with Inkscape. (Own work) [CC BY-SA 3.0], via Wikimedia Commons
41	1540	Society of Jesus (Jesuits) formed by Ignatius Loyola and six others	By ecastro (Flickr.com) [CC BY-SA 2.0], via Wikimedia Commons
41	1540	Brethren Church in the Netherlands now called Mennonites	By Jacob Burghart ([1] ([2])) [Public domain], via Wikimedia Commons
42	-	How the Roman Catholic Church Responded	Reformation Fire (9781781915219), Christian Focus Publications - Illustration by Jeff Anderson
44	1547	Edward VI, a Protestant, becomes king of England	By Unknown, scanned from Hearn, Karen, ed. Dynasties: Painting in Tudor and Jacobean England 1530-1630. New York: Rizzoli, 1995. ISBN 0-8478-1940-X., Public Domain, via Wikimedia Commons
44	1549	Book of Common Prayer published	Public Domain, https://commons.wikimedia.org/w/index.php?curid=557448
44, 49	1549	Book of Common Prayer published	Public Domain, https://commons.wikimedia.org/w/index.php?curid=55333163
44	1553	First Statute of Repeal	Antonis Mor [Public domain], via Wikimedia Commons
44	1572	St. Bartholomew's Day Massacre	Frans Hogenberg [Public domain], via Wikimedia Commons
44	1597	Christianity banned in Japan	By Kosei.S from TOKYO, JAPAN (TokyoGameShow010) [CC BY 2.0], via Wikimedia Commons
44, 48	1598	Edict of Nantes	Jan Antoon Neuhuys [Public domain], via Wikimedia Commons
45	1556	Thomas Cranmer executed for heresy	Author unknown [CC BY 4.0], via Wikimedia Commons
45	1559	Act of Uniformity	By Diliff - Own work [CC BY-SA 2.5], via Wikimedia Commons
45	1560	Geneva Bible published	By Classicalsteve - Own work [CC BY-SA 4.0], via Wikimedia Commons
45	1560	Scots Confession approved by Scottish parliament	
45	1562	Heidelberg Catechism	Author unknown [Public domain], via Wikimedia Commons
45	1563	Foxe's Book of Martyrs published	Author unknown [Public domain], via Wikimedia Commons
47	-	What about the Eastern Church?	By Grippenn - Own work [CC BY-SA 2.5], via Wikimedia Commons
48	1603	James VI of Scotland becomes James I of England	Daniël Mijtens [Public domain], via Wikimedia Commons
48	1611	King James Version of the Bible published	Earl McGehee-ShareAlike 2.0 Generic [CC BY-SA 2.0], via Flickr https://www.flickr.com/photos/ejmc/7311242798
48	1618	Synod of Dort	By Hove, G. van (http://www.entoen.nu/media/18_NationaleSynode.jpg) [Public domain], via Wikimedia Commons
48	1667	Milton's Paradise Lost published	By scanned by Marc Ryckaert (private collection) [Public domain], via Wikimedia Commons
48	1675	Pietism began by Philipp Jakob Spener	Author unknown [Public domain], via Wikimedia Commons
48	1675	Pietism began by Philipp Jakob Spener	By Phillip Jacob Spener [Public domain], via Wikimedia Commons
48	1678	Bunyan's Pilgrim's Progress published	Robin Drayton [CC BY-SA 2.0], via Wikimedia Commons
49	1618-1648	Thirty Years War	By Augusto Ferrer-Dalmau (Own work) [CC BY-SA 3.0], via Wikimedia Commons
49	1618-1648	Britain begins slave trade from Africa to Jamestown VA	By American Anti-Slavery Society (http://www.loc.gov/pictures/item/2008661294/) [Public domain], via Wikimedia Commons
49	1642	Civil War in England	By Charles Landseer (1799-1879) (User:Hajotthu) [Public domain], via Wikimedia Commons
49	1643	Solemn League and Covenant	Author unknown [Public domain], via Wikimedia Commons
49	1646	Westminster Confession of Faith	John Rogers Herbert [Public domain], via Wikimedia Commons
49	1646	Westminster Confession of Faith	By Westminster Assembly [Public domain], via Wikimedia Commons
49	1647	George Foxe founded The Society of Friends [Quakers]	Author unknown [Public domain], via Wikimedia Commons
49	1661	Sedition Act	By John Michael Wright - National Portrait Gallery: NPG 531 [PD-Art], [Public Domain], via Wikimedia Commons
51	-	George Whitefield	The Voice that Shook the World (9781845507725), Christian Focus Publications – illustration by Brent Donoho
52	1701	Society for the Propagation of the Gospel in Foreign Parts established	By from Angicans Online [Public Domain], https://en.wikipedia.org/w/index.php?curid=2003777
52	1707	Isaac Watts published his Hymns and Spiritual Songs hymnal	Author unknown [Public domain], via Wikimedia Commons
52	1721	Peter the Great imposed state control on the Russian Orthodox Church	[PD-UK-unknown, Public domain], via Wikimedia Commons
52	1730	Great Awakening began in American colonies	By J. Maze Burbank [Public domain], via Wikimedia Commons
52	1793	William Carey, first British missionary, begins his mission to India	Author unknown [Public domain], via Wikimedia Commons
52	1796	New York Missionary Society founded	By George Schlegel lithographers, [Public domain], via Wikimedia Commons
53	1739	George Whitfield & John Wesley preach the first evangelistic open-air sermons in England	Author unknown [CC BY 4.0], via Wikimedia Commons
53	1741	George Fredrick Handel composed the Messiah	Attributed to Balthasar Denner [Public domain], via Wikimedia Commons
53	1741	George Fredrick Handel composed the Messiah	By Novello Ewer & Company - Scanned from copy of manuscript in the British Library. [Public Domain], via Wikimedia Commons
53	1750	Age of Enlightenment took hold in European society	Joseph Wright of Derby [Public domain], via Wikimedia Commons
53	1764	Robert Raikes began the Sunday School Movement	By Daderot (Own work) [CC0], via Wikimedia Commons
53	1789-99	French Revolution	By inc (inc) [Public domain], via Wikimedia Commons
55	-	Praising God – John Newton	A Slave Set Free (9781781913505, Christian Focus Publications – Illustration by Jeff Anderson
55	-	Praising God – Fanny Crosby	The Blind Girl's Song (9781781911631), Christian Focus Publications – illustrated by Brent Donaho
56	1800	Revivals in Scottish Highlands and southern American states	Author unknown. Blisco assumed (based on copyright claims). [CC-BY-SA-3.0], via Wikimedia Commons
56	1807	Slave trade abolished in the British Empire, especially the Atlantic slave trade	London: John Murray, 1865. [Public Domain], via Wikimedia Commons
56	1807	Slave trade abolished in the British Empire, especially the Atlantic slave trade	By Karl Anton Hickel - Image: Bridgeman Art Gallery; Portrait: Wilberforce House, Hull Museum, Hull City Council [Public domain], via Wikimedia Commons
56	1845	Potato famine in Ireland	By User AlanMc on en.wikipedia [Public domain], via Wikimedia Commons
56	1849	All foreign missionaries expelled from Thailand	[Public domain], via Wikimedia Commons
56	1854	Pope Pius XI issued 'Immaculate Conception' dogma	By Alberto Felici (1871-1950) (Politisch Wissenschaftlicher Verlag Berlin, 1932) [Public domain], via Wikimedia Commons
56	1854	Spurgeon becomes pastor of New Park Street Church, London	By Alexander Melville (floruit in 1846, presumed dead by 1923) [Public domain], via Wikimedia Commons
57	1826	Glasgow City Mission	By John Lindie [CC BY 2.0], via Wikimedia Commons
57	1829	Plymouth Brethren church founded	By Gabimld - Own work, [CC BY-SA 4.0], via Wikimedia Commons
57	1835	Christians persecuted in Madagascar	By User:(WT-shared) Burmesedays, Perry-Castañeda Library Map Collection Madagascar Maps [CC BY-SA 3.0], via Wikimedia Commons
57	1837	Electric telegraph invented	Author unknown [Public domain], via Wikimedia Commons
57	1841	David Livingston arrived in Botswana	Author unknown [Public domain], via Wikimedia Commons
57	1842	Christian missionaries expelled from Ethiopia	By CIA [Public domain], via Wikimedia Commons
57	1844	YMCA founded in London	John Collier [Public domain], via Wikimedia Commons
58	-	Going Out Into All the World – Robert Moffat	Africa's Brave Heart (9781845507152), Christian Focus Publications – Illustration by Jeff Anderson
58	-	Going Out Into All the World – John Gibson Paton	[Public domain], via Wikimedia Commons
59	-	Going Out Into All the World – Hudson Taylor and the China Inland Mission	By Internet Archive Book Images [No restrictions], via Wikimedia Commons
59	-	Going Out Into All the World – Lottie Moon	Author unknown [Public domain], via Wikimedia Commons
59	-	Going Out Into All the World – Amy Carmichael with children	Author unknown [Public domain], via Wikimedia Commons
59	-	Going Out Into All the World – David Brainerd	A Love for the Lost (9781845506957), Christian Focus Publications – Illustration by Brent Donoho
60	1859	Charles Darwin published Origin of the Species	[Public domain], via Wikimedia Commons
60	1560-62	Revival in South Africa	[Public domain], via Wikimedia Commons
60	1861-65	American Civil War	By Thure de Thulstrup - This image is available from the United States Library of Congress [ID pga.04038, Public domain], via Wikimedia Commons
60	1865	China Inland Mission founded by Hudson Taylor	An Adventure Begins (9781781915264, Christian Focus Publications – Illustration by Jeff Anderson
60, 63	1865	Salvation Army founded by William Booth	Author unknown [Public domain], via Wikimedia Commons
60	1869	First Vatican Council	By ignote [Public domain or FAL], via Wikimedia Commons
61	1870	Jehovah's Witnesses founded	By Charles Taze Russell (Scan of the Cover of Watchtower magazine from 1907) [Public domain], via Wikimedia Commons
61	1871	Great Fire of Chicago destroys 50 churches and missions	Currier and Ives [Public domain], via Wikimedia Commons

Page	Timeline Year	Timeline entry / Section	Image license attribution
61	1873	Moody and Sankey begin their crusades	By Barron Fredricks, NYC. D11791 U.S. Copyright Office. [Public domain], via Wikimedia Commons
61	17873	Christianity legalized in Japan	Uchida Kuichi [Public domain or Public domain], via Wikimedia Commons
61	1879	Christian Science Movement Founded	Author unknown [Public domain], via Wikimedia Commons
63	-	Marching for God – Salvation Army Band, Charters Towers, ca. 1900	Author unknown [Public domain], via Wikimedia Commons
66	1900	Boxer Rebellion in China	By Torajirō Kasai [Public domain], via Wikimedia Commons
66	1908	Manchurian revival	By Greg Gordon [Public domain], via Wikimedia Commons
66	1929	Westminster Theological Seminary in Philadelphia founded	Used with the permission of the Archives of the Montgomery Library at Westminster Theological Seminary, Philadelphia PA
66	1931	HCJB radio station began in Quito, Ecuador	By Mschaa (Own work) [CC BY-SA 4.0-3.0-2.5-2.0-1.0], via Wikimedia Commons
67	1910	First World Missionary Conference	By 1910 World Missionary Conference (http://isae.wheaton.edu/projects/call-for-papers/) [Public domain], via Wikimedia Commons
67	1914-18	World War I	By Royal Engineers No 1 Printing Company. [Public domain], via Wikimedia Commons
67	1917	Russian Revolution [Communism begins]	Author unknown [Public domain], via Wikimedia Commons
67	1921	First church service broadcast on radio	By Djembayz (Own work) [CC BY-SA 4.0], via Wikimedia Commons
67	1924	NCRV, first international Christian radio station began in Netherlands	Author unknown [Public domain], via Wikimedia Commons
67	1925	Scopes Trial in America	Mike Licht-Attribution 2.0 Generic (CC BY 2.0], via https://www.flickr.com/photos/notionscapital/9650462984
67	1928	Pope Pius XI issued Mortalium Animos	By Vatican (Vatican) [Public domain,], via Wikimedia Commons
66	1929	Stalin becomes dictator in Soviet Union	Author unknown [Public domain], via Wikimedia Commons
70	1939-1945	World War II	By USAAF [Public domain], via Wikimedia Commons
70	1946/47	Dead Sea Scrolls discovered	Author unknown [Public domain], via Wikimedia Commons
70	1955	Banner of Truth magazine began	banneroftruth.org
70	1955-75	Vietnam War	By James K. F. Dung, SFC, Photographer - This media is available in the holdings of the National Archives and Records Administration,[(NAID) 530610, Public Domain], via Wikimedia Commons
70	1956	Jim Elliott Martyred	He is No Fool (9781845500641), Christian Focus Publications – Illustration by Neil Reed
70	1962-65	Second Vatican Council	Lothar Wolleh [CC BY-SA 3.0], via Wikimedia Commons
71	1948	World Council of Churches established	Abbie Rowe [Public domain], via Wikimedia Commons. National Archives and Records Administration, cataloged under the National Archives Identifier (NAID) 194177
71	1949	Billy Graham' first crusade	By Escapedtowisconsin Photo/Paul M. Walsh (Own work) [CC BY-SA 3.0], via Wikimedia Commons
71	1949	Chinese Communist Revolution	By The original uploader was Aukingluntom at Chinese Wikipedia [Public domain], via Wikimedia Commons
71	1950	Mother Teresa forms Missionaries of Charity Order	By Manfredo Ferrari (Own work) [CC BY-SA 4.0], via Wikimedia Commons
71	1951	Campus Crusade for Christ founded	By HandigeHarry (Own work) [Public domain], via Wikimedia Commons
71	1951	Campus Crusade for Christ founded	Prayitno-Attribution 2.0 Generic [CC BY 2.0], via https://www.flickr.com/photos/prayitnophotography/6291479824

Page	Timeline Year	Timeline entry / Section	Image license attribution
71	1951	Ruins of Qumran uncovered	By Tamarah (Own work), [CC BY-SA 2.5], via Wikimedia Commons
71	1955	Francis Schaeffer founds L'Abri	By Allan L. Winger (Own work), [CC BY-SA 3.0], via Wikimedia Commons
72	-	Important People in the Modern Church – Evangeline Booth	By Bain - Library of Congress, [Public Domain], via Wikimedia Commons
72	-	Important People in the Modern Church – John Murray	Used with the permission of the Archives of the Montgomery Library at Westminster Theological Seminary, Philadelphia PA
73	-	Important People in the Modern Church – Gladys Aylward	By The original uploader was Ibekolu at Chinese Wikipedia [Public domain], via Wikimedia Commons
74	1968	Jesus Movement begins	Attribution 2.0 Generic [CC BY 2.0], via https://c1.staticflickr.com/3/2777/4427928818_19a4985802.jpg
74	1971	The Hiding Place by Corrie ten Boom published	Author unknown [Public domain], via Wikimedia Commons
74	1974	First International Congress on World Evangelism in Lausanne	Florida Memory-Attribution 2.0 Generic [CC BY 2.0], via https://www.flickr.com/photos/floridamemory/11928157394
75	1980	World Evangelism Crusade in Seoul, Korea	Trailblazers – Billy Graham: Just get up out of your Seat (9781845500955), Christian Focus Publications – Illustration by: Allied Artists
75	1990	Collapse of communism	siyu-Attribution 2.0 Generic [CC BY 2.0], via https://www.flickr.com/photos/siyublog/1982035178

PULL-OUT TIMELINE – HEROES AND VILLAINS

Page	Timeline Year	Timeline entry / Section	Image license attribution
	1870-1847	Thomas Chalmers	By Stephencdickson (Own work) [CC BY-SA 4.0], via Wikimedia Commons
	CA 250-336	Arius	Author unknown [Public domain], via Wikimedia Commons
	CA 354-420	Pelagius	By Artaud de Montor (1772–1849) [Public domain or Public domain], via Wikimedia Commons
	1475-1521	Pope Leo X	Raphael [Public domain], via Wikimedia Commons
	1809-1882	Charles Darwin	Julia Margaret Cameron [Public domain], via Wikimedia Commons
	1889-1945	Adolph Hitler	By Heinrich Knirr (1862-1944) (http://www.dittatori.it/fotohitler2.htm) [Public domain], via Wikimedia Commons
	1925-2003	Idi Amin	By Archives New Zealand from New Zealand (Idi Amin's Speech Page 3) [CC BY 2.0], via Wikimedia Commons

KEY / LINKS FOR WIKIMEDIA COMMONS LICENSES:

CC BY 2.0	http://creativecommons.org/licenses/by/2.0	CC BY-SA 2.0	http://creativecommons.org/licenses/by-sa/2.0
CC BY 2.5	http://creativecommons.org/licenses/by/2.5	CC BY-SA 2.5	http://creativecommons.org/licenses/by-sa/2.5
CC BY 3.0	http://creativecommons.org/licenses/by/3.0	CC BY-SA 3.0	http://creativecommons.org/licenses/by-sa/3.0
CC BY 4.0	http://creativecommons.org/licenses/by/4.0	CC BY-SA 4.0	http://creativecommons.org/licenses/by-sa/4.0
		CC BY-SA 4.0-3.0-2.5-2.0-1.0	http://creativecommons.org/licenses/by-sa/4.0-3.0-2.5-2.0-1.0

CF4•K

TIMELINE: HEROES & VILLANS

Who's who: HEROES

These men and women represent those how have lived faithful lives to the glory of God and served the church well.

PAUL

Apostle of Jesus Christ, first missionary and writer of 14 books in the New Testament.

POLYCARP AND OTHER FIRST CENTURY MARTYRS

who chose death rather than deny the Lord Jesus Christ.

JEROME

made the first translation of the entire Bible into the common language of the people. It is called the Vulgate, which means 'common tongue'.

POPE GREGORY THE GREAT

was leader of the western church from 590-604. During that time he sent out missionaries throughout western Europe, wrote a preaching manual for priests and bishops and introduced Gregorian Chant, a new way of singing praises to God.

PETER LOMBARD

was a theologian and professor at Notre Dame University in Paris in the mid-12th century. He wrote The Four Books of Sentences, the first systematic (or organized system) theology textbook, which became a standard university text.

| *ca.5-64/67 | ca.70-155 | ca.342-420 | ca.540-604 | 1100-1160 |

BILLY GRAHAM

is an American evangelist who travelled all over the world preaching holding 'crusades' (large meetings) to preach the gospel.

DIETRICH BONHOEFFER

a German pastor was executed by the Nazis in 1945 for opposing Hitler and his policy to kill Jews, immigrants, the disabled, and anyone who did not conform to his idea of a 'perfect' person.

MARTYN LLOYD-JONES

was a Welsh minister, noted for being the greatest preacher of the 20th century. His written sermons continue to be read by many today.

CAMERON TOWNSEND

Wycliffe Bible Translators

founded Wycliffe Bible Translators in 1934 to send missionaries to tribes of people that had no written language. The missionaries learned the language, wrote it down and then translated the Bible for the people.

J. GRESHAM MACHEN

a New Testament scholar at Princeton Seminary, led conservative professors out of Princeton in 1929 because the Seminary had begun teaching wrong doctrine. He then founded Westminster Theological Seminary.

CORRIE TEN BOOM

Remembered today for saving many Jews from the Nazis by hiding them in her home.

| 1918- | 1906-1945 | 1899-1981 | 1896-1982 | 1881-1937 | 1892-1983 |

Who's who: VILLAINS

These men and women represent those who either taught false doctrine or tried to destroy the church.

MARCION OF SINOPE

was one of the first heretics who taught that the God of the Old Testament was not the true God. He was excommunicated.

ARIUS

a priest in Alexandria, began to teach in 320AD that Jesus was not the Son of God. This heresy has plagued the church for a long time.

PELAGIUS

was a heretic, who taught that there was no such thing as original sin. He said everyone is born good and then they choose whether to follow God or not.

MOHAMMED

was the founder of the Islamic religion, which directly opposes Christianity.

POPE LEO X

Excommunicated Luther because Luther refused to recant his criticisms of the wrong doctrines taught by the church leaders.

POPE PAUL III

Established the Inquisition to hunt down Protestants.

QUEEN MARY I

was a daughter of Henry VIII and a strong Catholic. She attempted to destroy the English Protestant church.

| 85-160 | ca.250-336 | ca.354-420 | 570-632 | 1475-1521 | 1468-1549 | 1516-1558 |

CHRISTIAN FOCUS PUBLICATIONS | © Linda Finlayson 2018 | Published by: Christian Focus Publications | www.christianfocus.com

THE MEDIEVAL CHURCH

COUNCIL OF CHALCEDON	FALL OF THE ROMAN EMPIRE	ANTHANASIAN CREED	COUNCIL OF ORLEANS	ETHIOPIAN MONKS TRANSLATE BIBLE INTO THEIR OWN LANGUAGE	BUBONIC PLAGUE	MOHAMMED, FOUNDER OF ISLAM, IS BORN	PSALMS TRANSLATED INTO ANGLO-SAXON	CHURCH DIVIDED INTO EAST AND WEST	BATTLE OF HASTINGS	FIRST CRUSADE	FOURTH LATERAN COUNCIL	MAGNA CARTA SIGNED BY KING JOHN

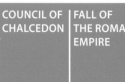

AD 315-500, page 18 · AD 315-500, page 18 · AD 315-500, page 18 · AD 497-1000, page 24 · AD 497-1000, page 24 · AD 497-1000, page 24 · AD 497-1000, page 25 · AD 497-1000, page 25 · AD 1000-1300, page 28 · AD 1000-1300, page 28 · AD 1000-1300, page 29 · AD 1000-1300, page 29 · AD 1000-1300, page 29

451 ▸ 476 ▸ 500 ▸ 511 ▸ ca.540 ▸ 542-594 ▸ 570 ▸ 700 ▸ 1054 ▸ 1066 ▸ 1066-99 ▸ 1215 ▸ 1215

THE MEDIEVAL CHURCH

AUGSBURG CONFESSION	MARBURG COLLOQUY	TYNDALE'S ENGLISH TRANSLATION OF THE NEW TESTAMENT PUBLISHED	LUTHER TRANSLATES THE NEW TESTAMENT INTO GERMAN	LUTHER EXCOMMUNICATED	LUTHER POSTS HIS 95 THESES AT WITTENBERG	MARTIN LUTHER BORN	JOHANNES GUTENBERG INVENTS THE PRINTING PRESS	COUNCIL OF CONSTANCE	WYCLIFFE BEGINS TO TRANSLATE THE BIBLE INTO ENGLISH	GREAT FAMINE IN EUROPE	SECOND COUNCIL OF LYONS	FIFTH, SIXTH AND SEVENTH CRUSADES

AD 1500-1530, page 36 · AD 1500-1530, page 36 · AD 1500-1530, page 37 · AD 1500-1530, page 37 · AD 1500-1530, page 37 · AD 1500-1530, page 36 · AD 1300-1500, page 32 · AD 1300-1500, page 32 · AD 1300-1500, page 33 · AD 1300-1500, page 33 · AD 1300-1500, page 32 · AD 1000-1300, page 28 · AD 1000-1300, page 28

1530 ◂ 1529 ◂ 1525 ◂ 1522 ◂ 1521 ◂ 1517 ◂ 1483 ◂ 1440 ◂ 1415 ◂ 1381 ◂ 1315-17 ◂ 1274 ◂ 1219-1248

MODERN CHURCH

WORLD WAR I	RUSSIAN REVOLUTION TURNS RUSSIA INTO A COMMUNIST STATE	FIRST CHURCH SERVICE BROADCAST ON RADIO	WYCLIFFE BIBLE TRANSLATORS FOUNDED	WORLD WAR II	DEAD SEA SCROLLS DISCOVERED	WORLD COUNCIL OF CHURCHES ESTABLISHED	BILLY GRAHAM'S FIRST CRUSADE	FIRST INTERNATIONAL CONGRESS ON WORLD EVANGELISM	NIV BIBLE PUBLISHED	COLLAPSE OF COMMUNISM	ESV BIBLE PUBLISHED

 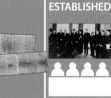 

AD 1900-1938, page 67 · AD 1900-1938, page 67 · AD 1900-1938, page 67 · AD 1900-1938, page 66 · AD 1939-1965, page 70 · AD 1939-1965, page 70 · AD 1939-1965, page 71 · AD 1939-1965, page 71 · AD 1966-2010, page 74 · AD 1966-2010, page 75 · AD 1966-2010, page 75 · AD 1966-2010, page 74

1914-18 ▸ 1917 ▸ 1921 ▸ 1934 ▸ 1939-45 ▸ 1946/47 ▸ 1948 ▸ 1949 ▸ 1974 ▸ 1978 ▸ 1990 ▸ 2008

THIS IS A SUMMARY OF THE TIMELINES FEATURED IN:

GOD'S TIMELINE

The Big Book of Church History

By Linda Finlayson

ca. before a date means that the date is approximate.

THE EARLY CHURCH

| JESUS DIES AND COMES BACK TO LIFE | PAUL IS CONVERTED ON ROAD TO DAMASCUS | COUNCIL OF JERUSALEM | APOSTLES PAUL AND PETER MARTYRED IN ROME | ROMANS DESTROY JERUSALEM | APOSTLES' CREED | FIRST MONASTERY FORMED IN EGYPT | COUNCIL OF NICEA | COUNCIL OF MILAN | COUNCIL OF HIPPO SETS THE CANON OF THE BIBLE | COUNCIL OF CARTHAGE | JEROME COMPLETES THE VULGATE | COUNCIL OF EPHESUS |

TIMELINE:

| AD 33-100, page 10 | AD 33-100, page 10 | AD 33-100, page 11 | AD 33-100, page 11 | AD 33-100, page 11 | AD 100-313 page 15 | AD 315-500, page 18 | AD 315-500, page 18 | AD 315-500, page 19 | AD 315-500, page 19 | AD 315-500, page 19 | AD 315-500, page 19 | AD 315-500, page 18 |

33 ▸ **34** ▸ ***ca.49** ▸ **64, 67** ▸ **70** ▸ **ca.180** ▸ **320** ▸ **325** ▸ **390** ▸ **393** ▸ **398** ▸ **405** ▸ **431**

REFORMING CHURCH

| SYNOD OF DORT | *KING JAMES VERSION* OF THE BIBLE PUBLISHED | JOHN SMYTH ESTABLISHES THE BAPTIST CHURCH | THIRTY-NINE ARTICLES FINALISED | HEIDELBERG CATECHISM | SCOTS CONFESSION APPROVED BY SCOTTISH PARLIAMENT | *GENEVA BIBLE* PUBLISHED | MARTIN LUTHER DIES | COUNCIL OF TRENT | HENRY VIII HAS ENGLISH BIBLE PLACED IN EVERY CHURCH | CALVIN PUBLISHES *THE INSTITUTES OF THE CHRISTIAN RELIGION* | ENGLAND BREAKS AWAY FROM THE ROMAN CATHOLIC CHURCH | LUTHER COMPLETES GERMAN TRANSLATION OF OLD TESTAMENT |

TIMELINE:

| AD 1600-1699, page 48 | AD 1600-1699, page 48 | AD 1600-1699, page 48 | AD 1547-1598, page 45 | AD 1547-1598, page 45 | AD 1547-1598, page 45 | AD 1547-1598, page 45 | AD 1532-1546, page 40 | AD 1532-1546, page 40 | AD 1532-1546, page 41 | AD 1532-1546, page 40 | AD 1532-1546, page 40 | AD 1532-1546, page 40 |

1618 ◂ **1611** ◂ **1609** ◂ **1571** ◂ **1562** ◂ **1560** ◂ **1560** ◂ **1546** ◂ **1545-1563** ◂ **1539** ◂ **1536** ◂ **1534** ◂ **1534**

REFORMING CHURCH   MISSIONARY CHURCH

| PILGRIMS LAND AT PLYMOUTH | CIVIL WAR IN ENGLAND | SOLEMN LEAGUE AND COVENANT | WESTMINSTER CONFESSION OF FAITH | GREAT AWAKENING BEGINS IN AMERICAN COLONIES | GEORGE FREDRICK HANDEL COMPOSES THE MESSIAH | AMERICAN DECLARATION OF INDE-PENDENCE | FRENCH REVOLUTION | SLAVE TRADE ABOLISHED IN THE BRITISH EMPIRE | POTATO FAMINE IN IRELAND | AMERICAN CIVIL WAR | CHINA INLAND MISSION FOUNDED | FIRST WORLD MISSIONARY CONFERENCE |

| AD 1600-1699, page 49 | AD 1600-1699, page 49 | AD 1600-1699, page 49 | AD 1600-1699, page 49 | AD 1700-1799, page 52 | AD 1700-1799, page 53 | AD 1700-1799, page 53 | AD 1700-1799, page 53 | AD 1800-1855, page 56 | AD 1800-1855, page 56 | AD 1856-1900, page 60 | AD 1856-1900, page 60 | AD 1900-1938, page 66 |

1620 ▸ **1642** ▸ **1643** ▸ **1646** ▸ **1730** ▸ **1741** ▸ **1776** ▸ **1789-99** ▸ **1807** ▸ **1845** ▸ **1861-65** ▸ **1865** ▸ **1910**

CHRISTIAN FOCUS PUBLICATIONS | © Linda Finlayson 2018 | Published by: Christian Focus Publications | www.christianfocus.com

RAMON LULL

was the first missionary to the Muslims.

ca. 1235-1316

JOHN WYCLIFFE

An English theologian who began translating the Bible into English.

ca. 1331-1384

JAN HUS

A Bohemian university professor and priest, who was influenced by Wycliffe. He urged his students and his congregation to worship God in their own language instead of Latin.

ca. 1369-1415

MARTIN LUTHER

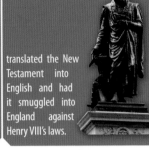

a university professor and priest, began the Reformation by questioning the pope's practice of selling indulgences.

ca. 1483-1546

WILLIAM TYNDALE

translated the New Testament into English and had it smuggled into England against Henry VIII's laws.

1494-1536

JOHN CALVIN

John Calvin, was a French pastor, church leader and theologian. He wrote *The Institutes of the Christian Religion* to instruct the church in the reformed faith.

1509-1564

CHARLES H. SPURGEON

was called the Prince of Preachers. 5,600 attended his church in London. He also started an orphanage, a charity home and a college to train pastors.

1834-1892

FANNY CROSBY

An American poet and hymn writer. Being blind did not stop her from writing over 9,000 hymns.

1820-1915

DAVID LIVINGSTON

arrived in Botswana in 1841 to begin work as a missionary and to explore the African continent.

1813-1873

WILLIAM CAREY

was first British missionary to India.

1761-1834

THOMAS CHALMERS

Leader of the evangelical movement in the Church of Scotland and first moderator of the Free Church of Scotland. Chalmers was an effective pastor, theologian, social reformer and passionate supporter of world missions.

1780-1847

GEORGE WHITFIELD AND JOHN WESLEY

preach the first evangelistic open-air sermons in England in 1739.

JOHN WESLEY: 1703-1791
GEORGE WHITFIELD: 1714-1770

LOUIS XIV

a French king, revoked the Edict of Nantes in 1685. Many Huguenots were killed and many others fled to other countries.

1638-1715

CHARLES DARWIN

published his book *The Origin of the Species* in 1859. The book is considered the beginning of the teachings of evolution, which denies creation of the universe by God.

1809-1882

MARY BAKER EDDY

Eddy founded the cult called Christian Scientism in 1879.

1821-1910

CHARLES RUSSELL

began the cult called Jehovah's Witnesses in the 1870s.

1852-1916

JOSEPH STALIN

had many Christians executed during the 1930s in an effort to purge the Soviet Union (Russia) because he wanted atheism to be the people's 'religion'.

1878-1953

ADOLPH HITLER

During World War II, Hitler had Christians as well as Jewish people arrested and sent to prison camps where many were executed or died of starvation.

1889-1945

IDI AMIN

Idi Amin reigned from 1971-1979 in Uganda, had over 40,000 Christians killed or kidnapped.

1925-2003

THIS IS A SUMMARY HEROES AND VILLAINS FEATURED IN:

GOD'S TIMELINE
THE BIG BOOK OF CHURCH HISTORY

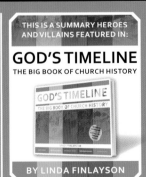

BY LINDA FINLAYSON

ca. before a date means that the date is approximate.